The Anthropological Turn

MORAL PHILOSOPHY AND MORAL THEOLOGY SERIES
Romanus Cessario, O.P., and Joseph W. Koterski, S.J.,
series editors

1. Martin Rhonheimer, *Natural Law and Practical Reason.* Trans. By Gerald Malsbary.

THE ANTHROPOLOGICAL TURN

The Human Orientation of the Theology of Karl Rahner

ANTON LOSINGER

Translated with a Foreword by
DANIEL O. DAHLSTROM

Fordham University Press
New York
2000

Copyright © 2000 by Fordham University Press

All rights reserved. No part of this publication may be reproduced, stored in a retrieval system, or transmitted in any form or by any means—electronic, mechanical, photocopy, recording, or any other—except for brief quotations in printed reviews, without the prior permission of the publisher.

Moral Philosophy and Moral Theology, No. 2
ISSN 1527-523X

Library of Congress Cataloging-in-Publication Data

Losinger, Anton.
    [Anthropologische Ansatz in der Theologie Karl Rahners. English]
    The anthropological turn : the human orientation of the theology of Karl Rahner / Anton Losinger ; translated with a foreword by Daniel O. Dahlstrom.—1st ed.
      p. cm. — (Moral philosophy and moral theology ; no. 2)
    Includes bibliographical references (p.) and index.
    ISBN 0-8232-2066-4 (hardcover)—ISBN 0-8232-2067-2 (pbk.)
    1. Rahner, Karl, 1904– . 2. Man (Christian theology)—History of doctrines—20th century. I. Title. II. Series.
BX4705.R287 L6713   2000
233′.092—dc21   00-044227

00 01 02 03 04 5 4 3 2 1
First Edition

CONTENTS

Translator's Foreword	vii
Foreword to the Second Edition	xv
Foreword	xvii
Preliminary Remarks: The Anthropological Point of Departure in the Theology of Karl Rahner	xix
Introduction	xxix

1. The "Anthropological Turn" in the Theology of Karl Rahner — 1
   - The Grounding of the Possibility and Necessity of the Anthropological "Turn" — 2
   - The Philosophical Background — 6
   - The Ambi-valence of the Point of Departure — 12

2. The Content of the Starting Point: Theology as Anthropology — 23
   - The Experience of the Self and the Experience of God — 25
   - Nature and Grace: The Intersection of Human Transcendentality and God's Communication of Himself — 35
   - God Becoming Human: Theology and Anthropology in the "Hypostatic Union" of the Event of Christ — 41
   - Overview: The Anthropologically Mediated Content of Theological Themes — 46

3. The Formal–Methodical Starting Point: Theology as Transcendental Reflection — 54
   - The Turn to the Subject — 59

Transcendentality and History	67
Overview: The Foundation of the Anthropological Point of Departure in Transcendental Theology	76
Excursus: On the Relation of Philosophy and Theology against the Backdrop of "Transcendental Revelation"	85
Postscript: Is Transcendental Anthropology the Adequate Form for Contemporary Theology?	91
Bibliography	95
Index of Names Cited	111

TRANSLATOR'S FOREWORD

Ever since the heyday of Enlightenment humanism, theology has found itself on the defensive. Hume and Kant hacked away at natural theology's proofs for the existence of a divine being and cast doubt on the reliability of revealed theology's historical claims. Mindful of the dualistic difficulties underlying Hume's and Kant's criticisms, German idealists responded by incorporating theology into a metaphysics based upon what they took to be emerging signs of an absolute within nature and history.

Yet there seemed to be something perversely wrong with the idealists' attempt to rescue theology, especially Christian theology, by strapping it down to a metaphysical lifeboat. On the one hand, as Kierkegaard quickly recognized, it became exceedingly difficult to see how such an all-encompassing metaphysical system—a dialectical system of pure thought or "esoteric contemplation of God," as Hegel also called it—could be reconciled with the existential reality implicit in such traditional theological concepts as revelation, the supernaturally transcendent, grace, and freely willed actions, both divine and human. On the other hand, as Feuerbach and Marx pointed out, the absolutistic pretensions of idealistic metaphysics reeked of Restorationist ideology, particularly in view of the fact that the Hegelian system of the absolute, conceived by its author as nothing less than the very justification of the Christian religion, seemed to give its blessing to an oppressive political-economic order. Hegel himself was, to be sure, a supporter of moderate, liberalizing policies within the Prussian state. Nevertheless, to those sensitive to the plight of the proletariat, there was no mistaking the fact that Hegel's true colors were not gray on gray, but the red, white, and black of the Hohenzollern.

For all the differences between them, Kierkegaard's and Feuerbach's criticisms of Hegelian theology together had the effect of exacerbating the problem of the viability of traditional theology, further riveting into Western culture an Enlightenment conviction that the study of God was inimical to legitimate science and genuine humanism. Before the century was out, this sentiment would be shared by even the severest critics of the Enlightenment and its aftermath. Thus, despite the fact that Nietzsche viewed the humanism of the likes of Feuerbach and Marx as little more than a diluted, closet Christianity, he joins forces with them on the issue of the anthropological deconstructibility of traditional theology. Nietzsche's views seemed to cast a spell on twentieth-century thinkers, and the same holds for his attitude toward theology, which ranges from bemused indifference to belligerent acrimony. On the one hand, he asks: "Who today still cares about theologians—other than theologians?" On the other hand, he declares war on the theological instinct that—unlike God—is far from dead: "I still dig up the theologians' instinct everywhere; it is a genuinely subterranean, infernal form of falsehood, the most widespread form of falsehood that there is on earth. What a theologian senses to be true, must be false; in this [observation] one has almost a criterion of truth."

In an important sense, as already noted, Nietzsche's disparagement of theology merely culminated more than one hundred and fifty years of hostility toward theology. Within this tradition, however, Feuerbach's savaging of religion is of particular significance for two important and complementary reasons. In the first place, as Nietzsche was fond of pointing out, Feuerbach's criticism was based upon a humanism that remained in agreement with certain key ethical principles of the Christian tradition. In the second place, that criticism effectively raised the critique of theology to another level, crossing the divide between theory and practice or, in other words, between the theologian's reflection and the experience of religion.

Having exposed the true colors of Hegelian metaphysics and its absolutistic theology, Feuerbach took the next step of asking whether the same dynamic is to be found in religion at large. Whereas Hume and Kant took direct aim at theology, Feuerbach's criticisms focused on the Christian religious experience that forms the basis of theological reflection. In a compelling thesis that would later be echoed by generations of Marxists and Freudians, Feuerbach argued that the essence of theology is anthropology. Religion, he contended, is nothing other than the projection of the complete fulfillment of the rational, volitional, and affectionate needs that are essential to the make-up of each human being as such, yet never fully realized in any one individual. Divine omniscience, omnipotence, and benevolence are, on this account, expressions of the dream of such fulfillment, an illusory satisfaction, yet one necessitated (at least for a time) by human indigence and alienation. Hence, Feuerbach concluded, the study of these expressions, traditionally understood to be theology, is in reality anthropology. Construed as anything else but anthropology, theology amounts, in Feuerbach's words, to the "false essence of religion."

Though the import of Feuerbach's charge should not be underestimated, his basic argument is problematic. He espouses a vague sort of naturalism and Marx rightly took him to task for its lack of a foundation in historical reality. Feuerbach's naturalistic conception of human nature, it turns out, is no less a theoretical projection than the rationalist theologian's conception of God. Moreover, he provides neither argument nor criterion for distinguishing false needs (such as, purportedly, religion) from true ones. Without such a criterion and adequate argument, the inference drawn by Feuerbach can be turned on its head. After all, in order for any single human being to exist at all, an entire constellation of needs must be met, only some of which rise to the conscious level of satisfied wants and desires. At some point each of us recognizes the truth—as mysterious as it is existential—that the presence of such natural, elemental, and radically individuated needs is matched, as long as we exist at all, by their fulfillment. Given this fact, it is perfectly natural and hardly unwarranted for human beings to assume that the presence of a need, especially to the degree that it seems elemental, entails the possibility of its realization. Why should the need for the divine be different? On what basis is it an unnatural, illusory need? Indeed, why should a need that surfaces in one way or another throughout the history of the species and in every corner of the globe ultimately prove to be a specious need?

Although Feuerbach did not make the case for his own conclusions adequately, he nevertheless put his finger on an obvious, though largely overlooked truth that theists and nontheists alike would have to take to heart. However theology and its validity be understood, they are inconceivable without taking into account the religious experience underlying theology and the conditions, in human nature, for that experience. Theology, in other words, is inconceivable without anthropology. The notion of a benevolent and merciful God, for example, is hardly meaningful without reference to the capacity of appreciating such love and, indeed, the need for it. In effect, a person's need for love and affection is part and parcel of her need for God and thus for the incipient theology built into reflection upon that need.

Faced with the challenge presented by the tradition of philosophical humanism stretching from Hume and Kant to Feuerbach and Nietzsche, the Christian theologian has no other option than to build into theological investigation a reflection upon the conditions in human nature for the experience of God and a relationship to God— cognitive and otherwise. The option is as welcome as it is necessary, since the Enlightenment argument that humanism and religion are intrinsically antithetical has not been sustained or has been sustained only in a dated, parochial manner. There is no reason for Christian theologians, especially in the wake of the political and cultural transformation of the world in the last century, to let atheistic, would-be humanists in the present presume that they have the high ground of the debate about what is in human beings' best interest because of some policies and doctrines adopted by the *premier état* a hundred or more years ago. At the same time, however, the Christian theologian can regain that high ground only by making the sort of transcendental and anthropological turn instituted by modern European philosophy.

Since, to be sure, in the theologian's view God must be the very source of the conditions of experiencing Him, there is an inevitable circularity to the theological argument. Yet this sort of circularity is not to be confused with a *circulum vitiosum*; indeed, far from being debilitating, it is a mark of the sort of consistency and adequacy found in certain classical philosophical arguments. Thus there is reason to think that the Platonic doctrine of recollection can only be articulated in a circular way, and the same arguably applies to the formulation of the Kantian unity of apperception. Since, as Kant insists, the "I think" must always be able to be affixed to any act of consciousness, it necessarily already obtains implicitly in any conscious act. A similar sort of structure is unmistakable in the phenomenological reflections of Husserl and Heidegger as well, whose analyses presuppose the capacity to render thematic some unthematic or horizonal dimension of experience that is originally lived, but not contemplated as such. A cognate structure also informs the argument of the theology that makes the transcendental and anthropological turn. The theological argument consists in establishing that and how God is the first principle (*principium*) in the *ordo essendi* through reflection upon the fact that divine being is necessarily, albeit unthematically intricated as the horizon-and-purpose (*Woraufhin*) of human being, the starting point (*initium*) in the *ordo cognoscendi* of the investigation.

The juxtaposition of the two adjectives 'transcendental' and 'anthropological' to characterize this turn in theology deserves some explanation. The term 'transcendental' in this context, despite its Scholastic roots, principally goes back to Kant, who used the term to designate knowledge, the object of which is a priori knowledge. Transcendental analysis is accordingly an attempt to isolate the conditions of the possibility of a priori knowledge such as that found, on Kant's view, in geometry. Eventually Kant expanded his transcendental philosophy to the realms of morality, aesthetics, and teleological judgments in general. Thus, he attempted to fix the a priori principles that human beings, as rational subjects, necessarily bring to the distinct realms of knowing, acting, and appreciating. Kant sets up his transcendental philosophy by directing his attention to the principles that respectively resolve the questions: What can I know? What should I do? and What may I hope for? Yet he himself observes that all three questions have an *anthropological* root, expressed in the question: What is a human being?

The preceding remarks have been made in an attempt to sketch how modern European philosophy has made a transcendental and anthropological turn in theological inquiry both conceivable and imperative. Such an inquiry would have to take its bearings from the genuine achievements of this turn in modern thought without surrendering its basis in faith and in the divine graciousness that is the source of faith. The aim of the following book is to introduce its readers to the way in which this sort of inquiry has, according to the author, been successfully carried out in the theological writings of Karl Rahner.

Enthusiastic, but not uncritical of Rahner's project, the author of the study, Dr. Anton Losinger of the University of Augsburg, pursues this objective in three carefully crafted steps. This first part of the study unpacks the *anthropological point of departure* in Rahner's thought by recounting, in particular, its philosophical background as well as the ambi-valence or complementarity of religious experience and religious mystery informing its anthropological turn. Losinger demonstrates how both Kant's transcendental philosophy and Heidegger's existential analysis serve as key sources of Rahner's project, without overdetermining it. In Chapter 2, devoted to the *content* prescribed by that point of departure, Losinger elaborates the sense in which theology and anthropology merge into one, as epitomized in the Incarnation. He elucidates their convergence by sketching the inevitable intersection of nature and grace, of experience of oneself and experience of God, and of human transcendentality and God's communication of Himself. Chapter 3 is concerned with the *method* of transcendental reflection dictated by the point of departure, in effect, a turn to the transcendentality and historicity of the subject. In a concluding excursus, Losinger traces the development of Rahner's thought from the earlier standpoint of *Hearers of the Word* to the revised, maturer position of *Foundations of Christian Faith*. He ends by posing some critical questions in need of resolution before transcendental anthropology can be regarded as an adequate form—or even the only adequate form—of contemporary theology.

Composed in admirably economical fashion, Losinger's study provides a useful, elementary introduction to the project of Rahner's theology. *The Anthropological Turn* demonstrates how, in the view of its author, Rahner manages to appropriate the transcendental and existential insights of modern and contemporary philosophy into a theological project in a way that does not undermine or defame but instead intelligently underscores and amplifies the mystery of faith. If Losinger is right, Rahner has effectively met the modern Enlightenment challenge, sketched in the preceding pages, by turning Feuerbach's thesis on its head. It is not the case that theology is reducible to anthropology, as Feuerbach insisted; but rather that anthropology, in the last analysis, is theology.

For their help and advice in translating *The Anthropological Turn* and in preparing the manuscript for publication, I am grateful to Anton Losinger, Michael O'Neill, Bernard Prusak, Mary Stephan Troxell, and Eugenie Schleberger.

The Catholic University of America
August 17, 1995

FOREWORD TO THE SECOND EDITION

The form and content of the study of theology in the present epoch are marked by a vast quantity of the most diverse and, at times, the most divergent points of departure. The classical unity and perspicuity of the world of theological thought, so typical for preceding centuries, has dissolved with the plurality of horizons and problems of modern thinking. The reality of the world, science, and theology no longer appears as a single "orbis," but rather as an open and unbounded space. Indeed, the catchphrase "a new vastness" thus appears to hold as well for the study of theology in modern universities.

This book is intended to provide interested Christians and theologians, especially students of theology, with an access to Karl Rahner; it is also intended to unpack his thinking and to make a theological inspection of his work possible. In this respect it is essential to locate the central point of departure for the theology of Karl Rahner in the concerns and questions of human beings and, taking cues from the key concept of the "anthropological point of departure," to make understandable the underlying tendency of Rahner's work.

Of necessity, mastering scientific inquiries in the everyday praxis of contemporary theological studies often takes the unsatisfactory form of a compilation of various essays, articles, and contributions to handbooks. Precisely for this reason, immersing oneself in the work of an epochally significant author, in the world of his thoughts, and in his theological profile—as here in the case of the theology of

Karl Rahner—ought to be, not only a dutiful exercise, but a delightful change of pace, perhaps even a passion—*studium* in the proper sense of the word.

Anton Losinger
Augsburg, April 1992

FOREWORD

The theological work of Karl Rahner is, without doubt, among the most impressive theological projects of the contemporary era. The reason for the far-reaching appreciation of his creative output most certainly lies in the nature of his response to problems and questions that have newly arisen as the order of the day in theology, problems and questions documented to some degree in his contributions to the *Quaestiones disputatae* and thematically arranged in the twenty-two volumes of his *Theological Investigations*. Occasionally, to be sure, Rahner's response has been unconventional, but in a time of considerable upheaval in the history of spirituality and the Church his farsighted response has pointed the way. But, to an even greater extent, his systematic draft of a transcendental theology and its "anthropological turn," as presented synthetically in the *Foundations of Christian Belief*, belongs to the lasting and fundamental achievements of the theology of the twentieth century.

During his entire life, it was always, to put it in terms of Romano Guardini's conceptual apparatus, the "concern for human beings" that moved Rahner to locate all theological inquiry and thinking in the human being and to provide an anthropological basis for all theological themes, from the doctrine of grace to that of the Trinity, from Christology to ecclesiology and sacramentology—all in the interest of providing them with their most original and appropriate meaning. By this means, an impulse was set in motion that led to the necessary disruption of theological positions that at times had become petrified. What is important, however, is not only the fact that this impulse with its far-reaching effects was set in motion at an historically significant juncture, namely, during the Second Vatican Council and the phase of its early reception. Above all, thanks to Rahner's anthropological turn, a useful bridge has been erected in the midst of the much-lamented situation of alienation in which the "Church in the Modern World" finds itself.

Anton Losinger
Augsburg, February 1991

PRELIMINARY REMARKS: THE ANTHROPOLOGICAL POINT OF DEPARTURE IN THE THEOLOGY OF KARL RAHNER

The history of thought places a considerable onus on anyone who sets out to do theology from an anthropological point of view. The main reason for this burden is the problematic antipathy that exists between theology and modern anthropocentrism, an antipathy that is rooted in the Enlightenment and its radical reinterpretation of both the image of the human being and the dimensions of reality as a whole.

At least since the time of the re-structuring of the entire edifice of Western thinking along singularly anthropocentric lines—a restructuring paradigmatically initiated by René Descartes and systematically carried out by Immanuel Kant—the question of God no longer forms the center of theological and philosophical systems. Instead, in an age of unimpeded critique of metaphysics, the new center of things is human consciousness assuring itself of itself. Along with several other inquiries and themes now of the same rank, the theological question of God henceforth circles around this new center like a satellite. The new *fundamentum inconcussum* ["unshaken foundation"] of the system of thinking is called "the subject" and the manner of thinking "autonomy."[1] With this new system of thinking the ideal foundations of a "critique of religion from the Enlightenment to the present" appear to be laid.[2] In this modern period of upheaval and criticism of religion, in the wake of Descartes's "*Cogito, ergo sum*" and Kant's *Critique of Pure Reason*, the names of Ludwig Feuerbach, Karl Marx, and Friedrich Nietzsche mark the foundations of a widespread conviction that any inquiry setting out from an anthropological point of view and rigorously questioning on humanity's behalf arrives at atheistic conclusions, namely, the overthrow of the divinity that, from the standpoint of the human being, is alienating: the "death of God" as a requirement for the "birth of the superman."

Hence, one might ask, is theology that sets out from an anthropological point of view not from the very beginning an absurdity, a *contradictio in se*, since modern anthropology after the Enlightenment is suspected (at times cavalierly) of necessarily pursuing the reduction of theology? On the contrary! "Precisely today," as Karl Rahner puts it in his article "The Theological Dimension of the Question of the Human Being," theology "must make contact with the human being whose own existence is of the utmost importance to him or her."[3] Thus, for Rahner that epochal and anthropocentric basic cast of mind in human beings' understanding of themselves today,[4] and no less, in anthropology as it is scientifically pursued,[5] signifies one of the most stubborn challenges and tasks for the contemporary orientation of theology. Yet this path urges itself upon us from the standpoint of theology itself. For the necessary anthropological dimension of the human being's question of God corresponds inversely to the "theological dimension of the question of the human being," postulated by Karl Rahner. If theology is understood as the question of God, a question or inquiry that in itself makes a demand of the human being in his or her entirety, confronting the human being with himself or herself, then theology inevitably places the inquiring human beings themselves in the middle of the inquiry. In other words, precisely because the question or inquiry is theological, it points directly and self-evidently to anthropology as the horizon and presupposition of theology. Thus, the basic possibility and legitimacy of an anthropological point of departure for theology become evident, on the one hand, and its urgency, on the other. Anthropology figures as the direct test of every theology, determining its character as well as its capacity to resolve the grave questions confronting humanity in the modern world.

On the Inquiry

In classical theological anthropology, the human being as a person,[6] as the entity that is *quoddammodo omnia* ("in a certain way everything"), forms the basis for the conception of an integrated anthropology, centered theologically in the measure of a divine likeness. The incomparable, inalienable, and utterly immeasurable dignity of a human being as the image and likeness of God is its foundation. The modern declarations of the rights of human beings correspond to this conviction and give it conceptual expression as a "justification of the individual in accordance with the dignity of the human being."[7] Although these declarations appear at a rather late date in the history of humanity, having been formulated in the age of Enlightenment, they document the uniqueness and incomparableness of the human person, possessing a dignity beyond all cultural and historical boundaries.

The anthropological starting point in theological thinking, presented here as it typically appears in the theological work of Karl Rahner, is, accordingly, to be understood not as a mere aspect of theology that deserves to be elaborated alongside other viewpoints. Instead, the anthropological starting point is to be understood essentially as theology's fundamental, dominant principle. Weaving like a red thread through the entire fabric of Karl Rahner's theology, it forms the sustaining criterion for the latter, responsible for the insight that it is precisely in the human being alone that the relevance of the divine can become obvious. To be sure, the object of hope is fulfillment, a fulfillment that happens only by the grace of God. But the hope for fulfillment is at the core of the human condition.[8]

If the unique position of the human being is thus really taken seriously, in contrast to all the misunderstandings of this position, epitomized by attempts to fix the boundaries of the preserves of theology and anthropology, then Rahner's demand for an "anthropological turn" in theology together with the "anthropological point of departure" implied by this demand appears as the only available and sensible path for theology. A theology that could not meet this stringent, anthropological claim would not only be a less valuable theology, but ultimately, in the face of modern questions, a theology of little use!

Sources and Secondary Literature

Traces of this starting point, corresponding to the basic, anthropological orientation of Rahner's entire work, may be found in all his writings.

The "early" major works, *Spirit in the World*[9] and *Hearers of the Word*,[10] already contain a kind of philosophical foundation for the "anthropological turn" in theology,[11] systematically unfolded in the essays compiled as *Theological Investigations*.[12] Worth mentioning here are, above all, the two articles "Theology and Anthropology"[13] and "Reflection on the Method of Theology."[14] The former drafts in a programmatic way the material dimension of an "anthropological starting point" of theology, whereas the latter explicates as a formal method the transcendental theological execution of this starting point. Finally, Rahner's *Foundations of Christian Faith* is to be understood as an example of developing a theology that sets out from an anthropological vantage point.[15] For the *Foundations* serves as the final edited position of this form of thinking, integrating corrections and suggestions of earlier, less mature works into a complete systematic presentation and thereby forming the "natural" reference point of the present study.

Some remarks on secondary literature are in order. As is quite understandable, a plethora of literature has accumulated in the course of time around Karl Rahner's theology. That literature is marked, on the one hand, by extremely uneven quality and, on the other, by a spectrum of assessments that extends from uncritical endorsement of Rahner's theology to emphatic attempts to repudiate it.

The present study deliberately makes no pretenses to any ostensibly "scientific" completeness in its consideration of secondary literature and, instead, makes use of a selection—in my view, a justified selection—of works on this theme that are recognized as fundamental.[16] Deserving mention in this connection are, above all, two more recent dissertations that assemble the previous lines of criticism and, each in a different way, critically engage Karl Rahner's anthropological point of departure. The first is P. Eicher's *The Anthropological Turn: Karl Rahner's Philosophical Path from the Essence of the Human Being to Personal Existence,* a work that aims at an explicitly philosophically oriented confrontation and engagement with Rahner's starting point.[17] The second is K. P. Fischer's *The Human Being as Mystery: The Anthropology of Karl Rahner.* In contrast to the formally philosophical analysis, what particularly matters for Fischer is a theological interpretation of Rahner's anthropology, one based on the latter's concept of mystery.[18] In the interest of completeness reference may be also made here to the helpful introductory works by K. Lehmann, H. Vorgrimler, and K. H. Weger.[19]

On the Method of Presentation

Given the position taken by the present study toward the theme of this investigation, an investigation that aims at setting forth the anthropological starting point in the theological thinking of Karl Rahner, the methodological decision about how to proceed is already settled. The theme of the investigation is to be approached from the perspective of theology. In keeping with the innermost sense and distinctive manner of Rahner's theology, this approach can in no way mean a neglect of the philosophical aspect, as will become clear in the course of the presentation.

The presentation aimed for here is a reflective analysis which in *synchronic* overview—in accordance with the method—is intended to uncover systematically those connections in the theology of Karl Rahner that identify it in its final form as a theology setting out from an anthropological vantage point. To a great extent the *diachronic* aspect may be left out of consideration, though it surfaces from time to time on the basis of marginal suggestions. In other words, what is not considered here is the methodical inquiry into (*a*) the manner in which this "anthropological turn" in the thinking of the author may itself have undergone an historical genesis from the first beginnings of his theology up to its final form—as is documented somewhat in the *Foundations of Christian Faith*—and, on the basis of that investigation, (*b*) the manner in which the anthropological turn must then be interpreted in a way immanent to the system but historically differentiated.

Notes

1. For an overview of both the place occupied by this autonomous manner of thinking as a point of departure within the

history of ideas and its importance, see the pertinent articles under the heading "autonomy" by R. Pohlmann in *Historische Wörterbuch der Philosophie*, ed. J. Ritter (Basel: Herder, 1971), 1: 701–19; E. Amelung in *Theologische Realenzyklopädie*, ed. Gerhard Krause and Gerhard Müller (Berlin: de Gruyter, 1980), 5: 4ff; and H. Blumenberg in *Religion in Geschichte und Gegenwart*, ed. Kurt Galling (Tübingen: Mohr, 1956) 1: 788ff.

2. For a valuable sketch of the most essential standpoints critical of religion since the Enlightenment, structured according to authors, cf. *Religionskritik von der Aufklärung bis zur Gegenwart: Autoren-Lexikon von Adorno bis Wittgenstein*, ed. K. H. Weger (Freiburg: Herder, 1979).

3. K. Rahner, "Die theologische Dimension der Frage nach dem Menschen," *Schriften zur Theologie* (Einsiedeln: Benziger, 1975), 12: 389. All volumes of *Schriften zur Theologie* have this same publisher and place of publication. Hence, hereafter reference is made solely to the volume, date of publication, and page number(s).

4. For a critical review of this modern consciousness of freedom in regard to its compatibility with theological principles of thinking after the Second Vatican Council, cf. A. Losinger, *Selbstbestimmung des Menschen und der Welt? Anspruch und Grenzen des Autonomiegedankens* (Cologne: Bachem, 1990) and *"Iusta autonomia": Studien zu einem Schlüsselbegriff des II Vatikanischen Konzils* (Paderborn: Schöningh, 1989).

5. For a thorough discussion of this matter, see *Neue Anthropologie*, Vols. 1–7, ed. H.-G. Gadamer and Paul Vogler (Stuttgart: Thieme, 1972–1974).

6. For a thorough account of this point, see J. Splett, *Der Mensch ist Person: Zur christlichen Rechtfertigung des Menschseins* (Frankfurt am Main: Knecht, 1978). In addition, see F. X. Bantle, "Person und Personbegriff in der Trinitätslehre Karl Rahners," *Münchener Theologische Zeitschrift* 30 (1979): 11–24; A. Halder, "Person. I. Begriffsgeschichte," *Lexikon für Theologie und Kirche*, 2nd ed., 8: 289ff., and, by the same author, "Anthropologie. I. Philosophische Anthropologie," *Staatslexikon* 7th ed., 1: 169ff.

7. The development of the idea of the rights of human beings in the context of the Enlightenment's postulate of freedom and the problematic history of its reception are demonstrated by J. Punt; see his *Die Idee der Menschenrechte: Ihre geschichtliche*

Entwicklung und ihre Rezeption durch die moderne katholische Sozialverkündigung (Paderborn: Schöningh, 1987), 11.

8. See J. Möller, *Die Chance des Menschen—Gott genannt* (Einsiedeln: Benziger, 1975), 266.

9. K. Rahner, *Geist in Welt: Zur Metaphysik der endlichen Erkenntnis bei Thomas von Aquin* (Innsbruck and Leipzig: Kösel, 1939; 2nd and 3rd eds.: München: Kösel, 1957, 1964). English translation: *Spirit in the World,* trans. William V. Dych, S.J. (London: Sheed & Ward; New York: Herder & Herder, 1968).

10. K. Rahner, *Hörer des Wortes: Zur Grundlegung einer Religionsphilosophie* (Munich: Kösel, 1941); revised edition by J. B. Metz (Munich: Kösel, 1963). English translation: *Hearers of the Word,* trans. Michael Richardo (London: Sheed & Ward; New York: Herder & Herder, 1969).

11. Various authors have already critically unpacked these philosophical foundations. Among the more significant works, the following deserve mention: E. Simons, *Philosophie der Offenbarung in Auseinandersetzung mit "Hörer des Wortes" von Karl Rahner* (Stuttgart: Kohlhammer, 1966); B. Lakebrink, *Klassische Metaphysik: Eine Auseinandersetzung mit der existentialen Anthropozentrik* (Freiburg i. Br.: Rembach, 1967). Noteworthy also is the very strident critique by C. Fabro in his *La svolta antropologica di Karl Rahner* (Milan: Rusconi, 1974). Recognized as the best presentation is, of course, P. Eicher, *Die anthropologische Wende: Karl Rahners philosophischer Weg vom Wesen des Menschen zur personalen Existenz* (Freiburg/Schweiz: Universitätsverlag, 1970).

12. K. Rahner, *Schriften zur Theologie,* 1–16 (1954–1980). English translation: *Theological Investigations,* 22 vols. (London: Darton, Longman & Todd; New York: Seabury/Crossroad, 1961–1993).

13. K. Rahner, "Theologie und Anthropologie," *Schriften zur Theologie* 8 (1967): 43–65. This article, which goes back to an address given by the author in 1966 in Chicago, is to be found in an expanded and thematically slightly different version in K. Rahner, "Grundsätzliche Überlegungen zur Anthropologie und Protologie im Rahmen der Theologie," *Mysterium Salutis* (Eisiedeln: Benziger, 1967), 2: 405–20.

14. K. Rahner, "Überlegungen zur Methode der Theologie," *Schriften zur Theologie* 9 (1970): 79–126.

15. K. Rahner, *Grundkurs des Glaubens: Einführung in den Be-*

griff des Christentums, 11th ed. (Freiburg: Herder, 1979). English translation: *Foundations of Christian Faith*, trans. by William V. Dych, S.J. (New York: Crossroads, 1993). Hereafter referred to as "Grundkurs," followed by the page number (with the corresponding page number of the English translation in parentheses). Note, however, that all Rahner quotations and other passages quoted in the text are original translations.

16. For an overview of the entire literature, see the bibliographies cited in the back of the present volume.

17. P. Eicher, *Die anthropologische Wende.*

18. K. P. Fischer, *Der Mensch als Geheimnis: Die Anthropologie Karl Rahners—Mit einem Brief von Karl Rahner* (Freiburg: Herder, 1974).

19. For the sake of completeness, a series of writings may also be indicated, writings that are not properly "scientific" but, even if from another perspective, nevertheless shed a not insignificant, clarifying light on the personality of Karl Rahner and the circumstances of many of the starting points of his thinking. Along with various interviews—such as "Gnade als Mitte menschlicher Existenz: Interview mit Karl Rahner," *Herder Korrespondenz* 28 (1974): 77–92; "Lebenslauf," *Der Entschluß: Zeitschrift für Praxis und Theologie* 31 (1977): 30–34, and "Erfahrungen eines Theologen: Karl Rahner über die Möglichkeiten und Grenzen der Theologie," *Herder Korrespondenz* 38 (1984), 224–30—the two following, illuminating volumes of conversations deserve special mention: *Karl Rahner im Gespräch*, vols. 1–2, ed. P. Imhof and H. Biallowons (Munich: Kösel, 1987). See also K. Lehmann "Karl Rahner. Ein Porträt," *Rechenschaft des Glaubens: Karl Rahner-Lesebuch*, ed. K. Lehmann and A. Raffelt (Freiburg: Benziger; Herder, 1979), 13X–49X; cf. also revised version: K. Lehmann, "Karl Rahner," in *Bilanz der Theologie im 20. Jahrhundert* ed. H. Vorgrimler and R. van der Gucht (Freiburg: Herder, 1970) 4: 143–80. And see H. Vorgrimler *Karl Rahner. Leben—Denken—Werke* (Munich: Manz, 1963) and K. H. Weger, *Karl Rahner: Eine Einführung in sein theologisches Denken* (Freiburg: Herder, 1978).

INTRODUCTION

"Today dogmatic theology must be anthropology and such an 'anthropological turn' is necessary and fruitful."[1] This programmatic demand at the beginning of his essay "Theology and Anthropology" displays with unmistakable clarity the point of departure and the basic conviction of Karl Rahner's theology. There is only one legitimate manner of pursuing systematic theology today; that is to complete that much-debated, but in Rahner's view absolutely indispensable "transcendental-anthropological turn" in theology, in other words, to look to human beings themselves with all their prejudices and limitations for the necessary and meaningful starting point as well as the ground of the possibility of every theological assertion. A theology that has made this "turn" and is anthropologically centered distances itself first, above all, from the outmoded method of arranging and treating the human being as a particular theme alongside, or even following, all other themes of theology. For the theology that is centered in anthropology radically breaks with the idea that "people can say something theologically about God without thereby also already saying something about human beings and vice versa; or that these two assertions are linked with one another only in reality, but not in knowledge itself."[2]

If theology and anthropology are thus originally and essentially coherent, as far as both the reality and the knowledge of things are concerned, then two complementary consequences follow. On the one hand, insofar as every theological assertion has to take its bearings from human self-experience and thus has to be a theology of experience, it must as a consequence be *anthropology*. On the other hand, it must be *transcendental theology* because it has to exhibit and acknowledge in transcendental reflection the conditions of the possibility, and therein the binding reference, of every instance of knowledge to the a priori structures of cognizing, human subjectivity.

Rahner's demands, in the form of a slogan, for an "anthropological turn" in theology accordingly imply a new "anthropological starting point" for theological thinking in two respects.

1. At the level of *content*, the human being is henceforth presupposed as the basic dimension and reference point of theological experience. Questioning that begins from anthropocentric and theocentric vantage points must no longer be understood as utterly and internally at odds with itself, but rather be taken seriously in reciprocally conditional and referential relations as ultimately congruent. For this reason, it is both possible and permissible to initiate and develop a theology in terms of its content as *theological anthropology*.[3]

2. At the level of *formal method*, theology is no longer carried out in the manner of traditional scholastic methods as the treatment of independent themes of belief *sic et simpliciter*. Rather, theology is pursued always in reference to and in the context of a transcendental reflection on the a priori conditions of the theological subject. This gnoseological conditionedness of theological knowledge establishes a transcendental theology which, as far as its epistemological point of departure is concerned, is rooted once again in the human being.

Obviously both these aspects, in unity with one another, form the "anthropological point of departure" in the theological thinking of Karl Rahner. For methodological reasons, of course, it is appropriate in the presentation to distinguish between a material and a formal dimension and to develop each apart from the other.

In any case, however, the "anthropological turn" in theology, postulated by Rahner, forms the basis and the presupposition for understanding such a point of departure. Accordingly, the first order of business is the elaboration of the foundation for this turn, its origins in the history of thought, and its internal problematic.

NOTES

1. Karl Rahner, "Theologie und Anthropologie," *Schriften zur Theologie* 8 (Einsiedeln: Benziger, 1967): 43.
2. Ibid.
3. For the thorough grounding of the co-extensiveness of both starting points, see K. Rahner, "Anthropozentrik," *Lexikon für Theologie und Kirche*, 2nd ed. (Freiburg: Herder, 1957), 1:632–34, and the tone-setting work of J. B. Metz, *Christliche Anthropozentrik: Über die Denkform des Thomas von Aquin* (Munich: Kösel, 1962).

1

The "Anthropological Turn" in the Theology of Karl Rahner

THE DEMAND that theology make an "anthropological turn," of the sort that Karl Rahner strives for in his work, continues to present one of the "most controversial topics" of theological research in the contemporary era.[1] Rahner's radical supporters contend that his work's epochal significance consists in the fact that it provides the only meaningful sort of theology at all, that is to say, the only kind of theology capable of facing the questions and demands of situations in today's world. Opponents see in it the greatest threat to contemporary Christianity; they warn of leveling tendencies in theology[2] and fear a dilution and even "anthropological reduction" of the Christian message.[3]

This concert of the most dissonant, contradictory voices challenges Rahner's justification of his basic position, his establishment of an "anthropological turn" for theology. In the face of this challenge, it is necessary, on the one hand, to demonstrate that the "anthropological turn" is vital and fruitful for the solution of the theological questions of the present without, on the other hand, giving rise to the suspicion that the fixed point of reference and core of any theology—God Himself—is ultimately abandoned here.

The Grounding of the Possibility and Necessity of the Anthropological "Turn"

Theology has traditionally been elaborated—as Rahner understands it—in the style of "objectivistically-deductive dogmatics." If one's aim is to pursue traditional theology in its entirety with anthropology as the point of departure and to consider all theological themes anew from this changed outlook, then it is possible to avoid the reduction of Christian belief only on one condition, namely, the firm establishment, from the outset, of the coextensiveness of anthropology and theology. For Rahner, in order to establish this coextensiveness, it is necessary to demonstrate a correspondence between the content of revelation and the a priori structures of the human capacity to comprehend things at all. The argument for this correspondence must begin first with theology itself and, from criteria immanent to theology, show how the turn is possible without slipping into some sort of inadmissable dependency in the form of a resort to extratheological foundations. In Rahner's theological project as a whole, it becomes clear that his fundamental goal is to free the anthropocentric impulse of the present from a theologically unacceptable, autonomous curtailment[4] and to put this impulse into a strict relationship with the fact that the human being is essentially constituted as a creature.

Leo Scheffczyk provides a starting point rooted in the thought that the human being is created in the image and likeness of God. For Scheffczyk what matters is a "relational-dynamic conception of the *imago dei* in the human being." In this theological conception the human being is accorded the status of being "the indicator of and the highest potential for the 'immediacy of God.'" On the basis of the theological premise "that the human being stands in immediate correspondence to God,"[5] it becomes possible to give a distinctly anthropological accent to the whole of theology. Only if there is a realization of the unambiguous relationship between theology and anthropology, and only if, "in the human being's act of responding to God and being that response or, to put it otherwise, in the human being's state of responsiveness or in a profound, religious-ethical 'responsibility' in the face of the absolute," there is a recognition that the essential potential of the human being is to enter into the "structure of the correspondence to the absolute Thou of God,"[6] then and only then is there nothing from a theological perspective standing in the way of the modern claim to anthropocentrism—as confirmed by Leo Scheffczyk, someone whose testimony is above suspicion on this question. Quite to the contrary, as he puts it: "From the standpoint of the doctrine of creation there can legitimately be something corresponding to the 'anthropological turn' in theology so much criticized today (according to which theology is supposed to be anthropology), even if a theological anthropology cannot be derived exclusively from the truth of creation. But it has its roots in that truth."[7]

As the foundation and presupposition for the "anthropological turn," a demonstration of the coextensiveness of the contents of anthropology and theology is obligatory. Rahner accomplishes this demonstration in a twofold manner, namely, in terms of the human being's salvation and in terms of the transcendental character of knowledge.

Human Salvation

The initial and directly theological consideration proceeds from the principle that every revelation is a revelation of salvation and every theology is, for that reason, essentially a theology of salvation. The content of revelation never includes anything arbitrary, but rather only what concerns the salvation of the human being. "That alone, however, can be a part of salvation, the lack of which harms the 'essence' of the human being and thus damns it. For otherwise an individual might, indeed, be able to renounce it, without thereby being damned."[8] Thus, it is possible, and it makes the utmost good sense, to pursue theology as "the illuminating way of leading everything that is significant for salvation back to this transcendental essence" of the human being.[9] In no way does this conviction imply a material derivation of the significance of salvation from that "transcendental essence," since every divine act of salvation must be realized and recognized in its a posteriori and contingent dimension, that is to say, in its historical underivability. Of necessity, however, this conviction presupposes that the entire theology of revelation—insofar as it must, at its core, be understood as theology of salvation—be referred back to a basic, a priori structure of the essence of the human being, a structure that is to be distinguished anthropologically.

Accordingly, the concept of the "transcendental essence," as it is introduced by Rahner in this passage, has to satisfy a twofold epistemological requirement. On the one hand, it must characterize the constitutive, theological vocation of the human being as the point of departure for the divine revelation of salvation. That is to say, it must make plain that unalterable core in the midst of the contingency of concrete human existence, a core which shows human existence to be necessarily and inevitably dependent upon the divinely mediated salvation, in an order that is both receptive to and comprehends human existence. On the other hand, that concept of the "transcendental essence" must emerge as a concept to be obtained in an inductively anthropological fashion from a transcendental analysis of the experience of human existence (*Dasein*). In philosophical reflection on the conditions of the possibility of human experience, fundamental anthropological constants of the "transcendental essence" will be able to be ascertained, "existentials," as it were, of human existence, existentially necessary properties which express that dependency upon divine salvation.

In the course of meeting both requirements, the only presupposition made is that the analysis of *Dasein* refer to questions, relations, and needs which are characteristic, in a central and constitutive manner, of what it means for the human being to be, regardless of whether the individual human being ever desires to have and admit them or not. For Rahner, according to K. H. Weger, such questions are chiefly questions of truth, freedom, guilt, love, fidelity, and even the human being's longing for salvation.[10]

Along with this genuinely theological grounding of the necessity of an "anthropological turn," oriented towards the concept of the mediation of salvation, Rahner also lists the following, more formal consideration.

The Transcendental Essence of Knowledge

It is of the essence of knowledge that, at bottom, there is an irreducible, uneradicable intersection of a subjective and an objective side. In every instance where the mind is said to know something, including the theological realm, the question of the object of knowledge also signifies from the outset a question of the horizon and the conditions present in the knowing subject. In the banal transactions with objects in the course of daily life, this question of the structure of knowledge belonging to the subject naturally does not ever need to be explicitly thematized. Yet the question is indispensable as soon as it is posited "as the question of the object in the whole of reality and truth as such,"[11] that is to say, as soon as the question of the ultimate grounds of objectivity in knowledge itself is posed in a genuinely philosophical sense. If from the outset, in the course of this sort of transcendental inquiry, the a priori conditions in the knowing subject must also be implicitly entertained as the foregoing horizon of the possibility of such knowledge in general, then analogously it may be inferred that this is the case for all theological knowledge. Every theological question is correctly posed only when at the same time, as a transcendental question, it attends to the cognitive horizon of the human mind as an internal factor and condition of its possibility, and thus presupposes itself. "Every such theology is, therefore, necessarily transcendental anthropology, every *onto*-logy is onto-*logy*," as Rahner puts it in his summary statement of this basic insight.[12]

The possibility and indispensability of this anthropological turning by theology can thus be made transparent on the basis of reasons immanent to theology as well as on the basis of general, philosophical considerations which follow from the essence of human knowledge.

The Philosophical Background

In order to show the suitability of Rahner's demand for an anthropological turn in theology, it is ultimately necessary to indicate how this point of departure originates in and is conditioned by its philosophical presuppositions and foundations.[13] For, indeed, before such a turn to the human being first surfaced in theology as a question, it had already been carried out for some time in philosophy. The question of the anthropocentric turn in the theology of the twentieth century has as its paradigm (and has its theoretical roots in) the anthropocentric turn of the philosophy of the Enlightenment during the seventeenth and eighteenth centuries.

From the time of René Descartes (1596–1650) at least, philosophical thinking no longer began with the objective reality "lying before" the mind. Instead, through a radical methodological doubt it sought in the self-certainty of the doubting-knowing subject the only secure truth from which all other certainties, including the existence of God, could be reliably deduced.[14]

This epoch-making segment in the intellectual history of the West, introduced by Descartes' recourse to the Cogito, reaches a high point in the establishment of the idea of a "transcendental philosophy" by Immanuel Kant (1724–1804), who carries out the revolutionary "Copernican turn" in knowing and thereby decisively seals the basic understanding of philosophy in modernity.[15]

Next to the unmistakable dependence of Rahner's thinking on the implications of transcendental philosophy, there is still a second root to his thinking, a root grounded in the existential ontology of Martin Heidegger (1889–1976).

In establishing the idea of a fundamental ontology—in an inquiry, critical of metaphysics, trying to get at what lies behind previous ontology—Heidegger understands being (*Sein*) in the case of the human being, as *Dasein*, in the modality of its existential condition as a caring "being-in-the-world." Heidegger reproaches all previous ontology with the "forgottenness of being" and, proceeding from this premise, follows a path that, on the one hand, consistently departs from an objectivistic view of being as an abstract, universal class of entities (*Seiendheit*), a view caught up in the leveling tendencies of an anonymous society, and, on the other hand, leads to human existence, an existence which, when comprehended in terms of the constitution of its existential necessity, must be the foundation of all further philosophizing.[16]

Transcendental reflection, on the one hand, and existential analysis, on the other, thus indicate the contours of Rahner's basic position as a theological application of elements of the modern view of the human being, articulated in the philosophical starting points of Kant and Heidegger. This application, however, does not mean that Rahner's position is no more than a mere adoption of structures that have been thought out before him. "While Rahner—in close correspondence to J. Maréchal—takes up Kantian thinking again and continues it in his own methodology, he demonstrates the possibility of making ontological assertions precisely in that way of thinking, in which this was presented as empty and a priori inaccessible. Rahner accomplishes this overturning [of the results of Kant's critique of dogmatic and speculative metaphysics] by taking over the point of departure of fundamental ontology, as it is to be found in Heidegger's early existential ontology."[17]

Immanuel Kant and the Transcendental Method

In the metaphysical tradition since the time of Plato, the question of knowing has been stamped by an intuitive identity of thinking and being, already postulated by Parmenides.[18] The ontological connection of *res* and *intellectus* within the *analogia entis*, that foundation of unity, without doubt permitted a certain naïve realism regarding knowledge. That naïve realism presupposed that, as expressed by the definition of truth as *adaequatio rei et intellectus*, being's opening of itself to knowing and the cognizing preconception of reality by the *intellectus agens* were in ontic and logical correspondence, that is to say, a correspondence making truth possible. *Ens et verum convertuntur*: This metaphysical first principle characterizes the essential relatedness to one another of mind and being in the epistemology of the philosophical tradition.[19]

Awakened by Hume from "dogmatic slumber," Kant in the *Critique of Pure Reason* begins his critical engagement with traditional metaphysics, an engagement characterized by the question: "How are a priori synthetic judgments possible?"[20] With this question Kant synthesizes what is otherwise a confrontation between the Cartesian-rationalistic conception of *ideae innatae* and English empiricism's opposing conception that all ideas of the mind stem solely from perception. All the elements of knowledge originating from the world are first realized in the knowing subject's a priori, foregoing horizon which is always already at work with those elements. Since the a priori forms of subjectivity constitute the objectivity of the object in knowledge, a correspondence reigns between the conditions of the possibility of the object and the conditions of its being rendered knowable. Consequently, the conditions of the possibility of the subjectivity that objectively knows are constitutive for the manner and type of knowledge itself. The knowledge of this link signifies for Kant a case of transcendental knowledge. "I call 'transcendental' all knowledge that is concerned not so much with objects but rather with our type of knowledge of objects insofar as this is supposed to be a priori."[21] Transcendental knowing essentially rests upon the transcendental subject's originally spontaneous act of positing the object. The famous "thing in itself" is, to be sure, necessary for thought, but not knowable.

For Rahner, it follows as a consequence, one that is both possible and legitimate, that the transcendental inquiry, as a method established by Kant, be taken up into theology. The inference is an acknowledgment of the inherence of all knowledge, even theological knowledge, in the subject and, thereby, an acknowledgment of knowledge's originally anthropological roots. The inference is thus not alien to the epochal self-understanding of the "human being in modernity." If the medieval form of thinking was spontaneously theological, the contemporary form is just as spontaneously anthropological!

Yet Rahner also distinguishes himself essentially from Kant. On the Kantian understanding of things, all knowledge is directed at something having the character of an object (*Gegenständlichkeit*: something standing over against the knower) and, for this reason, God and other complex ideas have no place in theoretical knowing, but rather first acquire reality as postulates of "pure practical reason."[22] By contrast, taking his cues from the Belgian theologian and philosopher, J. Maréchal, Rahner represents a much more broadly construed concept of knowledge, one that transcends the restriction of knowing to the objectivity of objects.[23]

Rahner's view of transcendentality, mediated in the direction of "objective" transcendence and first made possible on the basis of the latter, at the same time provides a condition for a vertical directedness of transcendental knowledge, in which metaphysical knowledge and even knowledge of God have a place. Moreover, Rahner constantly postulates a metaphysical unity of the transcendental subject in knowledge and freedom in contrast to the Kantian division of them, the radical separation of theoretical and practical reason, of knowing and acting.[24]

Martin Heidegger and Existential Ontology

Although Martin Heidegger's conception of an existential ontology, as he himself makes explicit,[25] departs from the plane of previous anthropology, his phenomenological analysis of *Dasein* understanding its being contains points of departure and ways of understanding that place the human being with its existential state of mind in the middle of things in a completely new manner. In contrast to objects, to the "readiness-to-hand" of the "totality of implements" and to the sheer "present-at-handness" of the theoretical objects of science, the human being has a constitutive "relation of being" toward the world, the human being, that is, as an historical entity that interprets himself or herself in temporality. "Being is thereby the formal existential expression of the being of *Dasein* that has the essential constitution of being-in-the-world."[26] *Dasein* is, existentially, care. That is to say that, of necessity, in the very way that it is constituted, *Dasein* always reveals itself to be referred to the world, caring and concerned, to be a thrown "being-along-with-things" and at the same time itself projecting that being.

The way from *Dasein* to being, as it is drafted in Heidegger's major work *Being and Time* in a manner that lays the groundwork for any fundamental ontology, is also a way referring back from being to *Dasein*'s understanding of being. "Thus, in the question '*ti to on*' there lies the more original question: what does the being that is already understood from the outset in the question mean?"[27] Phenomenological hermeneutics, in Heidegger's sense of the term, is conceived as the self-interpretation of the being that reveals itself in the existential accomplishment of *Dasein* as the being that understands being. For this reason, the aim of such a phenomenological hermeneutics is not to hold true only as a contingent, replaceable method or discipline for the analysis of *Dasein*. Rather, in accordance with its central claim, phenomenological hermeneutics is to be understood as the authentic perception of the "illumination" (that presents itself) of being itself,[28] the verification of which, for that reason, also prepares decisive moments and impulses for the new existential-anthropological self-understanding of the human being.

Heidegger's indisputable influence upon the work of Rahner, an influence that Rahner himself repeatedly acknowledges, is not limited solely to some conceptual points of reference such as Heidegger's treatments of themes like "state of mind," "existential," "accomplishment," "thrownness," and the like.[29] Rahner's inquiry, taking its start from the self-experience of the human being in the world, and its existential-anthropological interpretation, indicates instead more than a formal similarity with Heidegger's phenomenological analysis of *Dasein*. Above all, Rahner's interpretation also appropriates essential elements, when—deliberately expanding Heidegger's basic conviction—it takes the analysis of the existential structures of *Dasein* as its material origin. Rahner sees the conditions of an essential openness and reference to God on the part of the human being already laid out as a foundation in that analysis and accordingly turns to it to acquire the foundations of a phenomenology of the experience of God.[30]

Nevertheless, there is an essential distinction between the two thinkers. Rahner in the end does not enter into Heidegger's fundamental concern of clarifying the question of the meaning of being and the problem of a metaphysically critical fundamental ontology. Even the elementary difference between Heidegger's concept of *Dasein* and the modern concept of subjectivity, which is decisive for Rahner's thinking, was never discussed by him in a fundamental manner. A more nuanced presentation of the reception of Heidegger's thinking in the work of Karl Rahner may be dispensed with, given the particular context of this investigation's inquiry. For, despite all the dependencies on other thinkers, Rahner's thought moves at many levels and his theology ultimately remains determined by an ambi-valence that does not allow itself to be derived from philosophical influences.

The Ambi-valence of the Point of Departure

"In the beginning there is the human being, not some dogmatic assertion of belief."[31] In this way K. H. Weger pronounces his categorial judgment on Rahner's theology in his introduction to Karl Rahner's theological thinking. The point from which Rahner proceeds is, therein, not the dogmatic assertion of belief, but rather the "concrete self-experience of the human being today."[32] Rahner himself steps forward as the chief witness to the legitimacy of this judgment when he writes: "The grounding of belief may calmly begin with the human being. It is not to be feared thereby that the anthropological point of departure must necessarily lead to a subjectivistic or time-conditioned reduction of Christian belief."[33]

To be sure, H. Vorgrimler maintains the exact opposite in his evaluation of the place from which Rahner proceeds. In his introduction to the Festschrift that appeared on the occasion of Rahner's 75th birthday, Vorgrimler observes: "Your theology is the theology of the mystical experience of God, and anyone who would have wanted to attribute a transcendental-philosophical point of departure to it would have thoroughly misunderstood it."[34]

Vorgrimler appeals, moreover, to the testimony of Rahner himself: "The human being thus must become so determined as the essence of the mystery that this mystery constitutes the relationship between God and the human being, and, for that reason as well, the perfection of the human entity is the perfection of its being ordained to the remaining mystery."[35]

With the foregoing conflict of opinions we find ourselves in the middle of the problematic of providing an adequate intepretation of Rahner; that is to say, we find ourselves faced with the question: Is his a point of departure "from below" or one "from above"?

Experience or Mystery?

If one looks for an answer which recognizes Rahner's theology to be a theology of experience and takes seriously the fact that, in the wake of the philosophical fundamentals appropriated by it from Kant and Heidegger, it is referred back in transcendental-anthropological manner to the human being, the initial answer can only be: his point of departure is from below![36]

Nevertheless, the already cited work by K. P. Fischer,[37] which endeavors to demonstrate "mystery [to be] the original intuition of the theological anthropology"[38] of Karl Rahner, shows how much this point of departure is ultimately rooted in what descends "from above." Rahner—according to Fischer—takes his original bearings from mysticism, as is shown by his early essays in which he repeatedly and critically examined the central problem of mystical theories. Above all, however, his experiences with the Ignatian exercises revealed the "spiritual origin of his thinking,"[39] the ultimate theological realization of which is the *reductio in mysterium*.[40] These beginnings, rooted in the mystical experience of God, later became actualized in a fusion with the points of departure of modern philosophy, in which case, however, an "*ancilla*-function" was always attributed to philosophy over against the guiding thoughts of mysticism. In this way K. P. Fischer can maintain "that the discovery and introduction of the 'supernatural existential' signifies for Rahner a growing, theological relativizing of his philosophical concerns."[41]

Karl Rahner himself always spoke out energetically against a one-dimensional reduction of his theology. If the convenient point of departure from below forgets the mystery of God's reality grounding and finalizing everything, then it is just as questionable as a convenient point of departure from above, when the latter is taken as the sole principle of interpretation, in opposition to a theology of experience which takes its start in the respective "here and now" of the living human being.

"Thus, according to the general, everyday theological scuttlebutt I belong directly to the 'anthropocentric' theologians. That is, in the last analysis, absolute nonsense. I would like to be a theologian who says that God is what is most important, that we are here for this reason, to love him in a way that makes us forget ourselves, to leap out of the realm of our own existence into the abyss of his incomprehensibility. That a theologian must say that it is the human being who is finally related to God and must forget himself over God, that is naturally self-evident. In this sense one cannot pursue an anthropocentric theology enough."[42] Thus, Rahner's own depiction of himself and the point of departure of his theology.

The Mediation of the Points of Departure "From Above" and "From Below"

The contradictoriness of a one-dimensional interpretation of Rahner purely "from above" is immediately apparent when it is artificially placed in opposition to the transcendental-anthropological point of departure. For, in that case, to employ a musical comparison, the key is confused with the theme. In reality, the mystical experience of God and the anthropological turn of the theology of experience—setting out from the respective "here and now"—are, properly understood, not opposites, but instead two features of one and the same piece, reciprocally conditioning and interpreting each other. "Human being" and "mystery" are not mutually exclusive; they presuppose each other! This key observation immediately makes understandable the characteristic of Rahner's work that is so conspicuous from an external point of view, namely its "two tracks," the division into scientifically-systematic writings on the one hand, and spiritually-edifying literature on the other. At the same time, it delivers a final and very important reason for the legitimacy of the anthropological turn in theology. The central reason why it is possible to take one's point of departure "from below" is the fact that it has essentially been already "taken up"[43] in any point of departure "from above." In other words, the reason lies in the certainty of those who hope that, in all that they comprehend as they search for answers, they know themselves in a way that reveals that they are always already taken care of in the self-display of the absolute mystery, in the divinity of God Himself communicating with Himself.

Rahner accordingly understands the believer's existence as "the radicality of human rationality, assumed in its freedom, that is to say, when this rationality actually conceives itself as born and empowered by that transcendentality of precisely this rationality, in which the latter is lifted up into the mystery that is no longer comprehensible, the mystery that we call 'God' and with which, in the experience of that transcendentality, we cannot avoid having to be involved, whether we thematize this reference or not."[44] Hence, when Rahner understands the believer's existence according to this philosophical-conceptual definition, in the last analysis it essentially means nothing other than that contemplative prayer to be found in his "Words into Silence": "You have taken hold of me, I have not 'grasped' you; you have transformed my being from its ultimate roots and origins, you have made me part of your being and life . . . because you have, indeed, become the innermost center of my essence."[45]

From the standpoint of the theology of revelation, this connection means that the human being in her essential foundation is capable of, and called to be, a potential and actual "Hearer of the Word" of a divine revelation making its entrance into history. In the case of Rahner, this dialogical bond expresses itself in an emphasis on the transcendentally necessary dimension of Christian faith rather than on the moment of its historical contingency. Indeed, a basic question of the Christian proclamation of the faith, in the face of Enlightenment thinking, is the problem of the historical mediation of necessary truths, the so-called "Lessing problem" of any theology of revelation. This aporetic question of Christian apologetics is the question of how the Gospel message with its serendipitous entrance into history (which for that reason always bears in itself a trace of the historically "contingent") can lay claim to being universally valid and even necessary in a sacred sense. This question inevitably leads to an irresolvable contradiction between faith and thought if mediating criteria cannot be given which render the claim of the historically-categorial revelation evident and cogent for the a priori structures of thought. This question is at bottom one raised by the Enlightenment, and Rahner sees his conception of theology particularly challenged by it. The basis of the solution to this question lies in the transcendental mediation of revelation and history in the context of the anthropological turn of this theology. By this means, as remains to be shown, the insight into a novel "existential logic" is made possible, a logic articulated in the relation in which "categorial" and "transcendental" revelation distinguish and condition each other, a logic capable of bringing the act of revelation and the act of grasping it into a necessary unity that is mediated in a transcendentally a priori fashion. Because God Himself, by revealing Himself and at the same time graciously making possible the act of grasping Him, thus becomes the fixed point of the anthropological point of departure in theology, any question about the ambivalence of the starting points "from above" and "from below" ultimately becomes superfluous. Theology and anthropology have lost the appearance of being opposites. Faith and thought, the content of revelation and the knowledge acquired in modern sciences, overcome their alleged inconsistency with one another and converge on the basis of the common question of the human being.[46]

The fruitfulness of Rahner's point of departure within the context of systematic theology and at the same time its invigorating attractiveness against the horizon of the critical questions and pursuit of modern thinking may be traced to the fact that it gives piety and rationality each its due. It effectively treats both: ineffable mystery and the mundane, often banal experiences of everyday life. The human question in all its existential weight is taken seriously and, faced with the divine mystery, comes to expression in honest, theological form. At the same time, in the link that has already been shown, the mystical dimension is clearly renewed in Rahner's theology, a dimension that reaches its peak in the words often cited by Rahner: tomorrow's Christian will be a mystic or he will no longer exist at all.[47]

Notes

1. For this assessment see K. Lehmann, "Karl Rahner" in H. Vorgrimler and R. van der Gucht (eds.), *Bilanz der Theologie im 20. Jahrhundert* 4: 143–80, and J. B. Metz, "Karl Rahner" in *Ten-*

denzen der Theologie im 20. Jahrhundert, 2nd ed. (Berlin: Kreuz, 1967), 513–18.

2. See C. Fabro, *La svolte antropologica di Karl Rahner,* in particular the vehement criticism in the "Epilogus brevis," 202–4. Compare J. Ratzinger, *Einführung in das Christentum,* 3rd ed. (Munich: Deutscher Taschenbuch, 1977), 32; in additional detail, see Ratzinger's review of Rahner's *Grundkurs des Glaubens,* in J. Ratzinger, "Vom Verstehen des Glaubens. Anmerkungen zu Rahners *Grundkurs des Glaubens,*" *Theologische Revue,* 74 (1978), 176–86.

3. H. Urs von Balthasar, *Glaubhaft ist nur die Liebe,* 4th ed. (Einsiedeln: Johannes, 1975); Baltasar raises these issues here, especially on pp. 19–32: "Die anthropologische Reduktion."

4. A. Losinger, *Selbstbestimmung des Menschen und der Welt?,* 13–15, and E. Kleindienst, *Wege aus dem Säkularismus: Versuche zur Bestimmung des Weges der Kirche in säkularisierter Gesellschaft* (Donauwörth: Auer, 1991).

5. L. Scheffczyk, *Einführung in die Schöpfungslehre,* 3rd ed. (Darmstadt: Wissenschaftliche Buchgesellschaft, 1987), 109.

6. Ibid., 110.

7. Ibid., 99. Precisely in this connection, in the debate about the question of the possibility of a so-called "anthropological turn" of theology, one that would not ultimately be misconstrued through one of the several positions that distort it, L. Scheffczyk can be regarded as someone who supports the turn without becoming ensnared in those distortions.

8. K. Rahner, "Grundsätzliche Überlegungen zur Anthropologie und Protologie im Rahmen der Theologie," *Mysterium Salutis* (Benziger: Einsiedeln, 1967), 2: 409.

9. K. Rahner, "Theologie und Anthropologie," *Schriften zur Theologie* 8 (1967): 51f.

10. See K. H. Weger, *Karl Rahner: Eine Einführung in sein theologisches Denken,* 27.

11. K. Rahner, "Grundsätzliche Überlegungen zur Anthropologie und Protologie im Rahmen der Theologie," 408.

12. K. Rahner, "Theologie und Anthropologie," *Schriften zur Theologie* 8 (1967): 51.

13. For a study of Rahner with an explicitly philosophical orientation, see P. Eicher, *Die anthropologische Wende.* The first part of Eicher's work presents a thorough investigation of Rahner's philosophical dependence upon Kant and Heidegger.

14. On the ambivalence in the interpretation of Descartes between the outgoing, medieval-scholastic tradition and incipient modernity, as the founder of which he is loosely characterized, see J. Möller, *Die Chance des Menschen—Gott genannt*, 22–25. Möller refers especially to the ultimate, internal discordance in Descartes' thinking, which reveals itself in the diverse starting points of his proofs for God's existence.

15. I. Kant, *Kritik der reinen Vernunft*, B XIV: "Up until now people assumed that all our knowledge must orient itself to the objects; but all attempts to say something about them a priori through concepts, by means of which our knowledge would be expanded, have come to nought under these presuppositions. Thus, people might try it once [to consider] whether we do not advance further in the tasks of metaphysics by assuming that the objects must orient themselves to our knowledge...." The turn in knowing, characterized in this way, acquires its new point of reference in the transcendental subject and is compared by Kant with the thought of Copernicus.

16. In what follows an attempt is made to present Heidegger's idea of a fundamental ontology in the form of a sketch. Along with the "early" Heidegger's major work, *Being and Time*, the basis of the presentation is above all his study of Kant from the period before the so-called "turn" in his thinking. The study of Kant merits attention because it iterates Heidegger's critical engagement with the transcendental problematic and, by this means, becomes relevant for the reception of it by Rahner. The distinctive difficulties of the turn in the development of Heidegger's thinking can and need not be addressed in this connection. See Martin Heidegger, *Sein und Zeit*, 10th ed. (Tübingen: Niemeyer, 1963) and *Kant und das Problem der Metaphysik*, 3rd ed. (Frankfurt: Kostermann, 1965).

17. Eicher, *Die anthropologische Wende*, 4.

18. On the question of the historical influence [*Wirkungsgeschichte*] of Parmenides, the pre-socratic, within the Western metaphysical tradition, see, among others, J. Möller, *Wahrheit als Problem* (Munich: E. Wewel, 1971), 12–15.

19. This identity is unpacked by Thomas Aquinas in his *Quaestiones disputatae de veritate, Quaestio 1*, tr. A. Zimmermann (Hamburg: Meiner, 1986).

20. I. Kant, *Kritik der reinen Vernunft*, B 19.

21. Ibid., B 25.
22. For the grounding of this doctrine and its thorough presentation, see Möller, *Die Chance des Menschen*, 25–32.
23. Corresponding to this wider concept of knowledge, J. Maréchal writes in his major work, *Le point de départ de la métaphysique*: "Der kantische Agnostizismus . . . beruht auf einer zu ausschließlich formalen und statischen Auffassung der Erkenntnis, m.a.W. auf der Nichtbeachtung der dynamischen Finalität im Prozeß der objektiven Erkenntnis." The translation is cited according to L. B. Puntel, "Zu den Begriffen 'transzendental' und 'kategorial' bei Karl Rahner," *Wagnis Theologie. Erfahrungen mit der Theologie Karl Rahners*, ed. H. Vorgrimler (Freiburg: Herder, 1979), 196.
24. For a more extensive discussion of this point, see Chapter 3 of this work.
25. See M. Heidegger, *Kant und das Problem der Metaphysik*, 5–7. In an existential-ontological inquiry, in contrast to an anthropological investigation, the theme of interest is not the various accomplishments and forms of human beings, but rather the accomplishment of being-here (*Dasein*) itself and its relation to being, a relation consisting of *Dasein* interpreting itself in view of being.
26. Heidegger, *Sein und Zeit*, 54.
27. Heidegger, *Kant und das Problem der Metaphysik*, 201.
28. The "turn" in Heidegger's work implies a transformation of his viewpoint from the human being insofar as "essential thinking" is said to take place on the basis of being itself; in this manner, again by way of a criticism of metaphysics, every anthropological position is said to be broken through. In the present context, an adequate discussion of the problematic of this turn would lead too far afield and remains, in any case, of only secondary significance as an influence on Rahner's thinking. On this matter, see the extensive discussion in J. Möller's *Menschsein: Ein Prozeß* (Düsseldorf: Patmos, 1979), 136–37 and "Der späte Heidegger und die Theologie," *Tübinger theologische Quartalschrift*, 147 (1967): 383–431.
29. See K. Rahner, "Lebenslauf," *Der Entschluß, Zeitschrift für Praxis und Theologie* 31 (1977): 30–34, and R. Wisser, ed., *Martin Heidegger im Gespräch* (Freiburg: K. Alber, 1970), 48–50.
30. On the connection and the possibility of experience of

God in human self-experience, see K. Rahner, "Selbsterfahrung und Gotteserfahrung," *Schriften zur Theologie* 10 (1972): 133–44, and K. Rahner, "Gotteserfahrung heute," *Schriften zur Theologie* 9 (1970): 161–76.
31. Weger, *Karl Rahner*, 23.
32. Ibid.
33. K. Rahner, "Glaubensbegründung heute," *Schriften zur Theologie* 12 (1975): 24.
34. H. Vorgrimler, "Ein Begriff zur Einführung," in *Wagnis Theologie: Erfahrungen mit der Theologie Karl Rahners*, 13. For the systematic explication of the context of this interpretation which proceeds from the theological starting point of the mystical experience of God, see especially the groundbreaking work by K. P. Fischer, *Der Mensch als Geheimnis. Die Anthropologie Karl Rahners—Mit einem Brief von Karl Rahner*.
35. K. Rahner, "Über den Begriff des Geheimnisses in der katholischen Theologie," *Schriften zur Theologie* 4(1967): 68.
36. This philosophically oriented manner of interpretation is pursued by P. Eicher in his *Die anthropologische Wende*.
37. Fischer, *Der Mensch als Geheimnis. Die Anthropologie Karl Rahners*.
38. Ibid., 209.
39. Ibid., 17.
40. Ibid., 232–34.
41. Ibid., 45. Fischer provides a pointed résumé of Rahner's thinking, as just sketched, with a view toward a predominance of theology over philosophy; cf. ibid., 44–45.
42. P. Imhof and H. Biallowons (eds.), *Karl Rahner im Gespräch*, 2: 166.
43. The concept "taken up" (*Aufhebung*) must be thought of here in Hegel's sense in the threefold significance of the term as *tollere, elevare*, and *conservare*.
44. K. Rahner, "Die theologische Dimension der Frage nach dem Menschen," *Schriften zur Theologie* 12 (1975): 399.
45. K. Rahner and H. Rahner, *Worte ins Schweigen—Gebete der Einkehr*, 5th ed. (Freiburg: Herder, 1980), 34–35.
46. The aporie and the beginning of a solution to this fundamental question of theology are shown by J. Möller in his *Glauben und Denken im Widerspruch? Philosophische Fragen an die Theologie der Gegenwart* (Munich: E. Wewel, 1969), especially

59–79: "Begegnen sich Theologie und Philosophie im Gott-Sagen?"

47. For an overview of the question of the basic mystical lines in Rahner's theological work, in particular that of the problem of the interference of the divine mystery and transcendental theology, see K. P. Fischer, "Wo der Mensch an das Geheimnis grenzt: Die mystagogische Struktur der Theologie Karl Rahners," *Zeitschrift für Katholische Theologie* 98 (1976): 159–70; K. Kienzler, "Geheimnis Gottes und Transzendentaltheologie. Karl Rahner," in *Religionsphilosophie heute*, ed. A. Halder, K. Kienzler, and J. Möller (Düsseldorf: Patmos, 1988), 162–68; M. Krauss, "Einweihung in das Geheimnis. Anmerkung zu Karl Rahners Theologie," *Quatember* 43 (1979): 90–94 and "Vom Urgeheimnis, das wir Gott nennen. Karl Rahner begeht den 80. Geburtstag," *Lutherische Monatshefte*, 23 (1984): 101–3.

2
The Content of the Starting Point: Theology as Anthropology

ALTHOUGH RAHNER—probably under the influence of the spirituality of Ignatian mysticism—searches for the foundations of his "anthropocentric turn" completely within the framework of theology and on its basis, the realization of this starting point nevertheless implies, as a logical consequence, a move in the direction of anthropology. The move is theologically as well as philosophically motivated. It has already been demonstrated in Chapter 1 that there is a way of mediating the two starting points of theological thinking, "from above" and "from below," starting points that were previously considered opposites. In accordance with this mediation Rahner claims that the concept of the "theonomy" of the human essence cannot mean something essentially different from human experience, but rather that precisely in this theonomy the basis of a human being's experience of himself or herself is expressed. As K. H. Weger observes in the course of elaborating this fundamental feature of Rahner's theology: "All theological questions, understood in the proper sense, begin with the question of God; all other theological questions are 'only' ways of unpacking this one question, while the question of God must begin with the question of the human being."[1]

Anthropology accordingly stands at the beginning and in the center of every responsible theology. For anthropology first gives adequate expression to the fact that the human being is the basic dimension and point of reference for every theological assertion; it thematizes the essence of the human being as that incomprehensible entity in which the whole of reality comes to consciousness. Within Karl Rahner's theological framework, this mediation of the points of departure may be seen on three thematic levels:

1. The philosophical *self-experience of the human being*, where it is probed in its depths and its foundation, necessarily presupposes from the outset the unlimited horizon of a transcendental openness and, therein, the basis for the possibility of the theological *experience of God*. The subjectivity and transcendentality of the human being are at bottom reciprocally related just as are self-experience and the experience of God.

2. In the context of the dogmatic inquiry regarding *nature and grace*, human nature is always thought of as centered in the "supernatural existential" of God's communication of Himself, an existential which essentially gives the human being the capacity for the "immediacy of God."

3. Finally, in the sacred history of the fact of God's becoming human, the hypostatic union through the incarnation of the *Logos* in Jesus Christ—to put it in terms of dogmatic concepts—the divine-human *communio* takes place in the full sense of the word and makes it possible for Christian theology to take its start, as far as its central content is concerned, from anthropology.

Anthropocentrism and theocentrism thus ultimately come together in a single unity, reciprocally conditioning and making each other possible in regard to the central "objects" of belief. Because "theocentrism, rightly understood, is transformed into anthropocentrism through the grace that God Himself communicates,"[2] a theology of this sort, that takes its start from anthropology, will not overlook the essence of Christianity or degrade the concept of God's divinity by subjecting it to the limitations of human finitude. For it is also true that "the human being in turn can only find himself if, praying and loving, he lets himself go into the free incomprehensibility of God, thus transforming his very anthropocentrism into theocentrism."[3]

Accordingly, the "anthropological point of departure" in Karl Rahner's theology legitimately acquires its content and justification in its necessary and systematic recourse to the human being's experience of himself or herself and, what is substantially implied by that experience, the beginning of an experience of God.

"THE EXPERIENCE OF THE SELF AND THE EXPERIENCE OF GOD"[4]

In the inevitable relationship in which a theological and an anthropological understanding of the self stand, the anthropological dimension of the question of the human being is broached properly only when it is viewed in its necessary unity with the theological dimension of the same question. The theological dimension of the question first becomes apparent precisely when a human being experiences herself, that is to say, when she is brought before herself as an individual and as a whole, and in that experience cannot avoid contemplating the fact that she is exposed to and referred to the infinite, the inconceivable. That a human being can have an experience of this sort (an experience of transcendental necessity, that he or she, as the case may be, must accept) is revealed by the fact that, in the act of denying and refusing it, the act is itself implicitly affirmed and its unavoidableness acknowledged. Even in the repression of the notion of oneself as a whole and as free, in the existential phenomenon of not-wanting-it-so, it is still the individual human being who acts, knows, and wants. Because she becomes for herself a question and therein inevitably opens up the necessarily unlimited horizon of such questioning, she has already in some way grasped herself and posited herself as an entity that is more than the sum of contingent individual moments, moments even arbitrarily substitutable for one another. "Precisely this condition of being-brought-before-himself, this confrontation with the totality of all that conditions him, demonstrates that he is more than the sum of the factors composing him."[5] They show him to be precisely the sort of being that from the outset is always handed over to himself and, at the same time, drawn away from himself in the experience of his dependence upon the ever greater whole, the incomprehensible mystery of God.

If, in this way, the human experience of the self and what from the outset is always, albeit unthematically, given with that experience, namely, the human being's experience of God, are perceived in their unity, as postulated by Rahner, then two significant conclusions follow for theological knowledge.

1. Every experience of God is an occurrence in the subject, in which this subject at the same time is also given to itself and experiences something essential about itself. For this reason the experience of God necessarily has its basis in the human being's experience of himself or herself and is a substantial feature of the latter. There exists, therefore, an indissoluble unity and reciprocity between the experience of God and the experience of the self, in the absence of which neither experience would be able to be understood at all and each would lose its own respective significance.

2. With this unity, however, an absolute identity is not given, since, in the first place, the subject of the human experience of the self is radically different from what we experience as "God." In the second place, even in the purest truth of the subjective experience of the self, the subject ultimately remains finite in contrast to the infinite absoluteness of the transcendental mystery. "The unity

consists rather in the fact that the original experience of God is a condition of the possibility of the experience of the self as well as a moment of it, that no experience of the self is possible without the experience of God, and, furthermore, that the history of the experience of God thus signifies the history of the experience of the self."[6]

This observation is also valid when formulated precisely in reverse. "The experience of the self is the condition of the possibility of the experience of God, because a dependence upon being in general and thereby upon God can only be given, where the subject is given to itself (precisely in the preconception of being in general) in contrast to its act and the object of the act. Accordingly, it can just as well be said that the history of the experience of the self is the history of the experience of God."[7]

Given his acknowledgment of this principal and, as far as any theological question is concerned, elementary relation of the reciprocity between the experience of God and the experience of the self, what matters to Rahner is the following task. In a transcendental analysis of the experience of existence,[8] initiated by modern philosophy with its focus on subjectivity, he sets out to make transparent that personal and subjective, essential structure of the human being, which from the outset always places it in a transcendent openness to the absolute.

The Human Being as Person and Subject

"As far as the presuppositions for the message of the revelation of Christianity are concerned, the first thing that is to be said about the human being is this: the human being is a person, a subject."[9]

Each individual empirical science, in keeping with the epistemological method of the respective discipline, starts with a destructive phase, breaking the human being down into various elements. Then, in a constructive phase, it arbitrarily puts those elements back together into a functional unity. In contrast to the regional and particular sketch of human beings presented by these sciences, the human being experiences herself more fundamentally and more comprehensively as an original totality and unity subsisting in herself. The fact of her "being-able-to-relate-to-herself" and "having-to-deal-with-herself"[10] is not simply one feature alongside others in the experience of reality, but instead radically sets her apart from the nature of all other objects. Because a human being "always is concerned with more and has to deal with more than the things that people speak about in words and concepts and that they are preoccupied with as the concrete object of their actions here and now,"[11] she constitutes and conceives herself precisely as an "original self-possession," as a personal subject. When, in the very foundation of her existence, the human being experiences herself as an original, indissoluble unity, as a "whole handed over" to herself,[12] given in freedom and responsibility, it is something that cannot be derived, something no longer "capable of being produced" from available elements; a human being is a person and a subject in the proper sense of the term. "To be a person thus means a subject's self-possession as such in being referred, knowingly and freely, to the whole."[13]

Such a concept of subject and person is of fundamental importance for the essence of Christianity. "A personal relation to God, a dialogical salvational history between God and the human being, the reception of one's own, unique, eternal salvation, the concept of a responsibility before God and His judgment—all these assertions presuppose this basic datum."[14] Without adequate concepts of "person" and "subject," it is not possible to make such assertions understandable.[15]

Because Rahner from the outset conceives each human being, in his or her personal subjectivity with all the finitude of that horizon, always in view of his or her respectively greater totality, the next, theologically necessary step is already evident. A human being's subjective, personal consciousness is only possible and understandable in an already given and preconscious surmounting of everything finite, even his or her own experience of finitude, in the experience of transcendence. The subjective character of the human essence first becomes clear, in the final analysis, when the human being is conceived and determined as the essence of transcendence.

The Human Being as the Essence of Transcendence

All knowledge of the finite in its finitude presupposes a foregoing knowledge of the infinite, even though the latter knowledge is not reflexively thematized, just as a previous experience of the value of the absolute is the condition of the possibility of freedom as the capacity to choose between finite values. For this reason, this fact of being placed between finitude and infinity is what constitutes being human. "Human beings demonstrate themselves to be entities with an infinite horizon since, as soon as one of them posits the possibility of a merely finite horizon to a question, this possibility is overtaken in turn. Because a human being experiences its finitude so radically, its reach passes beyond this finitude and it experiences itself as the essence of transcendence, as spirit."[16]

This phenomenon of the personal subject being opened, a priori, to transcendence not only expresses itself as a particular capacity of the human being, but shows itself in the radical way the human being achieves, carries out, and perfects her personality, in the way that, as a self, she perfects or brings to completion her essence in knowledge and freedom. It is given as an experience precisely then, "when the human being, caring and concerned, fearing and hoping, experiences herself exposed to her everyday world in all the latter's diversity."[17]

Because the human being is thus set out into the "open" through this transcendental movement, Rahner overcomes what he characterizes as the "original sin" of modern philosophy, namely, that transcendental legacy that grew out of the Kantian negation of any metaphysical knowledge, the "fall in which a subjectivity that is closed off within its own individuality makes itself independent without transcending itself towards God."[18] The concept of such an autonomously isolated subjectivity is radically deconstructed by Rahner since transcendence is ultimately not determined as the self-positing of a subject "absolutely" conceiving itself, but rather in the sense of a receiving of meaning and, by the same token, a bestowing of meaning by the transcendent ground of the movement of transcendence. The movement of transcendence is accordingly "not some powerful act by which a subject is said to constitute its own infinite space as though it were absolutely in control of being, but rather the ascendancy of the infinite horizon of being from this horizon itself."[19]

Already in *Hearers of the Word*, Rahner takes some early steps towards a solution to this problematic of transcendence. In his concept of the "preconception" (a concept influenced by the analysis of knowledge in *Spirit in the World*), the cognizing "being-with-itself" of the spirit becomes the guiding anthropological concept of *Hearers of the Word*.[20] "The human being is spirit"[21] is the basic definition of the human being's essence, a definition that thereby implies the conviction "that the absolute openness for being belongs without qualification to the basic constitution of the human being."[22] The "transcendence of knowledge," a transcendence that in prereflective, preconceptual fashion seizes upon "being in general,"[23] determines the human being as a spiritual entity in such a way that, in the self's never-ending movement "towards being in general," it is always aware that individual objects that it knows also make the moments of this motion possible, since it regards them from the outset in view of the horizon by means of which each human being is always already open for the absolute being of God. In its prereflective grasp of being, the human being spiritually carries out the act of being itself and, by this means, is also at the same time always carrying out the act of transcending, moving into the foregoing openness of the divine infinity. "The human being is the spirit, that is, it lives its life in a constant extending of itself towards the absolute, in an openness to God."[24]

While human consciousness, in the course of abstracting and conceiving, is intent upon being among individuals, it finds itself from the outset referred to the general horizon of the objectivity of individual things, to the spiritual, a priori "forestructure" of knowledge in each instance. This forestructure, as far as the complete way in which it makes things possible as a whole is concerned, is ultimately grounded in spirit's dynamic movement of transcendence. The preconception is thereby "a capacity, given a priori with human nature, a capacity for the dynamic self-movement of spirit in the direction of the absolute expanse of all possible objects."[25] By way of summing up these points, Rahner writes in the *Foundations of Christian Faith* as follows: "The human being is the essence of transcendence insofar as all her knowledge and acts of knowing are grounded in the preconception of 'being' in general, in an unthematic, but ineluctable awareness of the infinity of reality."[26]

This analysis may be developed purely hypothetically into a "transcendental proof of God's existence." Of more interest in this connection, however, are its anthropological implications. The preconception decisively constitutes the person with the result that the human being, if he questions himself in the ultimate depths of his person, appears as the very "essence of transcendence," that is to say, as "that entity to whom the unavailable and mute infinity of reality constantly dispatches itself as a mystery. By this means the human being is rendered utterly open to this mystery and, precisely as a person and subject in this sense, is confronted with himself."[27]

As the anthropological result of the transcendental analysis of the experience of *Dasein*, the following insight must accordingly be retained. The first condition of the possibility of that experience lies in the human being as the subjective pole of the existential experience of the self. At the same time, however, this experience of the self always also refers, from the outset, to the constitutive, transcendent ground that makes it possible, characterizing the human being as something that, in its very essence, is "referred to the holy mystery . . . so that the human being in a real sense is 'more' than it is."[28]

The "Horizon" of Transcendence as the "Sacred Mystery"

If, according to this anthropological understanding, the human being is in a real sense a subject and, thereby, in an equally real sense the very essence of transcendence in knowledge and freedom, then that also means that, as entrusted to himself and handed over to himself, he always points to the unavailability of his transcendent ground. As the entity referred to God, the human being is at the same time constituted, retrospectively and prospectively, by the final ungroundability and unavailability of the "horizon" of its movement of transcendence. Rahner identifies the absolute horizon of liberating and loving transcendence, defying and eluding limitation and determination by means of names and concepts, as the "sacred mystery." "If, therefore, lovingly free transcendence goes towards the horizon that itself opens up this transcendence, then we can say that the unavailable, nameless, absolutely availing dominates in loving freedom, and it is precisely this that we mean when we say 'sacred mystery.'"[29]

The background concept of mystery, as Rahner understands it, is only appropriate for the essence of the transcendental experience of the infinite sending itself, an essence that precludes any definition. He describes it in a way equal to the "silently distant presence" of the ineffably sacred. "In transcendence, then, the nameless and infinitely sacred pervades in the mode of the unavailed and availing, impenetrable distance."[30]

In the final analysis all other concepts are grounded in this transcendent mysteriousness, however clearly they immediately present themselves; all clear conceptualizing is grounded in the obscurity of God. As the experience of the infinite mystery, the thus characterized transcendental experience is, from the outset, an unthematic experience of God, "in which that which we call 'God' is always giving silent assent to the human being—giving that assent precisely as the absolute, incomprehensible, as the horizon of this transcendence, a horizon that cannot genuinely be moved into some system of coordinates, and a transcendence that, as the transcendence of love, also experiences this very horizon as the sacred mystery."[31]

If, on the basis of this experience and as an anthropological consequence, the human being is understood in its essential transcendence as the "essence of the sacred mystery," then that implies at the same time that God, as the sacred, is essentially given to the human being. As K. P. Fischer has expressed the matter, the human being is conceived in this relation as the "loving ecstatic entrance into the mystery."[32]

Standing in the background of this anthropological conception is Bonaventure's doctrine of the "ecstasy of the spirit" at the apex of the soul, the *apex mentis* at least according to what Fischer has emphasized. If one proceeds from this vantage point, then Rahner appears to have understood the *itinerarium mentis ad deum* as the "spirit turning inward, into itself (*reditio in seipsum*) towards its highest point where, beyond conceptual knowledge, it is excess—that is to say, where it transcends itself and moves into the mystery of God that has drawn near. At this point, the *apex mentis* where the human being borders on the divine mystery, it necessarily also becomes a mystery to itself, because it is caught up and enveloped by the obscurity of the divine presence."[33] In this light there appears, Fischer is convinced, the most central sentence in Rahner's anthropology: "Being a human being means being referred to the absolute mystery"—leading the entire human transcendentality back to love as "the capacity of assuming something unquestionably greater, of being oneself seized, of submitting and giving oneself, of loving ecstasy."[34]

It is possible to question the extent to which Bonaventure's *Itinerarium mentis in Deum* (*The Mind's Journey to God*) legitimately provides the basis for leading the human being back to love in the manner stated, as well as whether this interpretation adequately lays out Rahner's project of the *reductio in mysterium*.[35] Answering these questions, however, oversteps the limits of the sort of methodological inquiry that has been the aim of this study from the beginning, namely, an inquiry into the roots of Rahnerian theological anthropology; moreover, addressing these questions would demand a separate investigation. In this connection it is important merely to point out the "mystical" meaning in which Rahner's philosophical anthropology reaches its peak and, thereby, at its profoundest juncture, sets itself apart from all the anthropological projects of comparable philosophical currents, projects that, in their immanence, are closed off from the mystical reach of Rahner's thought. In the context of Karl Rahner's theology it remains decisive that the *mysterium*, for all the ways that it continues to be withdrawn and unspeakable, is never understood solely as a sheer magnitude "in itself," as a *mysterium stricte dictum*, but rather always in a twofold relation. On the one hand, it is the "mystery of the human being"[36] relative to the human knowing that is receptive to it and takes it in; on the other hand, however, it remains the mysterious, gratuitous self-showing of the incomprehensible and, at bottom, unspeakable God.

For Karl Rahner's theology and spirituality, this elementary dichotomy of human existence, the identity yet irretrievable difference between the scientific, theological reflection and the divine mystery, has been a challenge and task of the first rank. Karl Lehmann characterized his teacher in this tribute to Karl Rahner immediately after his death on March 30, 1984:

> Even in his profoundest reflections, this theologian never allows himself to forget from the outset the irretrievability of the concrete act of living and the irreplaceability of lived faith by scientific knowledge. In the very heart of this spirituality there lives a great passion for the immensity and incomprehensibility of what we call "God." Again and again Rahner's theology draws its entire dynamic from this ever vital spring; again and again it breaks apart the crusts of all theological concepts and constantly finds its way back into an inexhaustible mode of thinking, of meditation, of spiritual and theological discourse, that rejuvenates those concepts. This fundamental experience is also the reason why, from the very beginning and even into the final developments of his thinking, Karl Rahner was able to preserve the great themes of the classical *theologia negativa* as, indeed, the decisive element of the life of his thinking: the ignorance of God and God as the "mystery."[37]

NATURE AND GRACE:
THE INTERSECTION OF HUMAN TRANSCENDENTALITY AND GOD'S COMMUNICATION OF HIMSELF

Any theology that takes anthropology as its point of departure is confronted with a basic problem. As has already been suggested, that problem consists in the precarious incongruence and potential for internal discontinuity between the structures of a priori, human subjectivity (that have been articulated from an anthropological point of view) and the contents of revelation (that have been posited from a theological point of view). The latter in their factual, historical givenness are no more acceptable empirically than the elements of the so-called "nature" of the human being that have been formally obtained on the basis of an analysis of *Dasein*. In his determination of the relation of nature and grace, Rahner attempts to bring both sides into a mediating unity. Because grace, as the expression of God's communication of Himself, becomes the constitutive core of nature and because the "natural" existence of human beings is, for that reason, at the same time radicalized and lifted up in the "supernatural existential" of God's grace, what is theologically self-evident and what is anthropologically self-evident come into immediate proximity to one another. In K. H. Weger's view, "the anthropological starting point of theology, as it is attained with the help of the transcendental method," thereby finds "an unmistakable high point in Rahner's concept of the 'supernatural existential.' "[38]

Grace as the "Supernatural Existential" of the Human Essence

At first glance the formulation of this central concept of Rahner's theology suggests a contradiction, thereby giving expression to the relation, in itself ambivalent, of nature and grace to one another. In connection with the concept of the "existential" coined by Martin Heidegger in *Being and Time*, Rahner has recourse to the phenomenological constitutedness of *Dasein* as "being-in-the-world," thus to a determination of its being which is "naturally" appropriate to this *Dasein* and characterizes its existence.

With the same necessity the concept of the "supernatural" is coordinated with the constitutive "natural" determination of the human essence. The purpose of the concept of the supernatural is to thematize what has been bestowed upon the subject, namely, its openness and orientation to the ever greater reality of God and grace. Finally, on the basis of this transcendental reality, the possibility of the establishment of the immanent reality can first be derived. In the relation constituted by grace,

"grace is at the same time a reality that is given to such a degree in the innermost core of human existence in knowledge and freedom, and so given, always and everywhere, in the mode of an offer, in the mode of taking it up or refusing it, that a human being cannot at all step out of this transcendental peculiarity of its essence."[39]

Thus, given the way that the human being is transcendentally constituted, a constitution that is always from the outset predispositioned by grace, a human being is never only a "purely" natural human being, but rather always a human being standing under the reality and dynamics of divine grace. Grace is the reality which "existentially" determines each human being's basic state of mind and finalizes it in the direction of the transcendent goal: God. What is innermost in the humanly *natural* Dasein becomes *supernaturally* constituted, corresponding to the scholastic axiom: *Gratia supponit et praedisponit naturam.*

Accordingly, in the determination of the essence of the human being as a "supernatural existential," two elements are always combined into a definitively inseparable totality. On the one hand, if grace is understood as the "vocation of the spiritual subject as such to the immediacy to God,"[40] the natural a priori structure of human subjectivity always remains a presupposition and material basis for the act of grace. It remains a presupposition and material basis precisely insofar as "nature, understood as something personally-spiritual and transcendental, is an internal, constitutive, necessary aspect, not, to be sure, of grace as such, but of the reality and the process in which grace can actually be given."[41]

Yet in order to be able to assume God's existence and take Him up into one's own humanity without thereby necessarily "disempowering" Him and demoting Him to the level of humanity's own finitude, the "transcendental nature" of the human being requires a foregoing radicalization and surmounting of human transcendentality, effected by God, through the free and gratuitous gift of grace. In this process, God Himself becomes the innermost, constitutive principle of the subject of faith, though He is at the same time the content of the revelation for the subject and shares responsibility for the act of listening in the subject as the basis of that act through His own communication of Himself as the *momentum movens*. Hence, in what transpires here, along with the material content of God's assent and offer of Himself in grace, at the same time "the acceptance must be borne by God Himself, even though God's communication of Himself as offered to the human being is also the necessary condition of the acceptance of it."[42]

The divine self-communication is mediated on the same plane as is the relation, constituted by this communication, between God and the finite entity. According to Rahner's conception of the matter, this plane presents itself in the supernatural existential: the dynamic, necessary, gracious vocation and determination of the human being to be "the immediacy to God," a determination that remains as something offered to the human being even in the latter's act of refusing it. At the same time, a bridge is thereby established between theology and anthropology, a union which legitimizes and makes possible the anthropological point of departure for theological inquiry in the human experience of the self, legitimizing it and making it possible on the basis of a horizon that is always shaped in advance by the transcendental revelation of grace—even if there is no conscious reflection on that horizon in the respective experience. The "heart and soul" of this bridge-building between theology and anthropology is the "supernatural existential."

In this conception with its foundation in the theology of grace, the human being is regarded in his significance as the subjective pole of the theological relation of grace and realized in his immediate and unavoidable relevance as a necessary, mediating, and mediated "quantity" of the act of revelation.

The Radicalization of the Human Essence as the "Immediacy to God"

As far as the contents and dimensions of it are concerned, the constitution of human transcendentality by grace, formally grounded—as shown above—in the "supernatural existential," signifies a radicalization of the human essence to the point of being the "immediacy to God." From a factual standpoint that means nothing other "than the fact that the transcendental movement of the spirit in knowledge and freedom towards the absolute mystery is shouldered by God Himself in His communication of Himself in such a way that this movement has its aim and its source, not in the sacred mystery as some ever distant goal, only asymptotically attainable, but rather in the God of absolute nearness and immediacy."[43]

The cause of this finalizing of the creature to be in the immediate nearness of God lies, above all, in the fact that God in His communication of Himself does not effect and posit anything in the creature arbitrarily different from Himself, but rather gives His assent to the finite subject in His own divine reality and thus in "quasi-formal causality"—as Rahner calls it—becomes the constitutive ground of the finite subject's existence.[44] "The giver is himself the gift"[45] and gives Himself through Himself to the creature. That means then: "The essence and the sense of this communication by God of Himself to the spiritual subject, so understood, consist in God's becoming immediate for the subject as something spiritual, hence, in the fundamental unity of knowing and loving."[46]

In the supernatural existential, by virtue of the fact that the human being is basically constituted by grace, he or she first becomes a radicalization of his or her respective self-elaboration and self-perfection in knowledge and the free activity of the self. Thus, too, he or she is placed in the immediate nearness of God Himself. In this fundamental sense, it is valid to affirm that "the human being is the event of God's communication of Himself."[47]

Hence, because human experience of the self, in its ultimate profundity, is based upon the "supernatural existential," it is always also a transcendental experience of God[48] and at the same time a transcendental experience of grace. Since, however, "the radicalization of all dimensions of anthropology and of the human being itself . . . signifies what we call God," and since at the same time "grace produces nothing other than the radicalization of the essence of the human being,"[49] it can be set up as a basic principle that "God's communication of Himself," graciously underlying the "supernatural existential," is "a modification of our transcendentality as such, a modification radicalizing it to the extreme."[50]

In Karl Rahner's conception of transcendental theology, then, the formally philosophical transcendental analysis is from the outset always concerned with the a priori structures of human subjectivity as they are formed by grace. As far as its method is concerned, this anthropology begins in philosophical fashion, but it is nevertheless carried out in what is, in principle, a transcendentally theological way. As such, it clearly situates itself in a way coextensive with the "fact" of divine relation and demonstrates therein its capacity to be completely and legitimately integrated into theology. Thus, it is securely established that "the light of faith as a supernatural existential is also always part of a human being's adequate, a priori self-understanding and that, for this reason, the human being does not oppose a posteriori anthropology with some a priori norm that is alien to theology."[51]

The danger of an anthropological reduction of theology is thereby completely removed and excluded, at least as long as one takes adequately into account the grace-imbued and theonomical constitution of human transcendentality as well as the gnoseological consequences that follow from this. Thus, as a theologically grounded method, the transcendentally anthropological form of inquiry proves its efficaciousness in the realm of the theology of grace. "Without an ontology of the transcendental subject, a theology of grace (and thereby theology in general) remains stuck in a state of pre-theological picture-thinking and cannot exhibit the rudiments of a transcendental experience."[52] Thus, in the last analysis, it becomes apparent that "this transcendental turn in the theology of grace signifies such a turn for the whole of theology."[53]

GOD BECOMING HUMAN: THEOLOGY AND ANTHROPOLOGY IN THE "HYPOSTATIC UNION" OF THE EVENT OF CHRIST

"The human being exists on the basis of God's communication of Himself and towards that communication."[54] This elementary proposition of Karl Rahner's theological anthropology can, on the basis of the preceding presentation, be understood as the foundation and mediating criterion of a theology that takes anthropology as its point of departure. God's promise and offer of Himself to human beings, grounding their existence, is ultimately not merely a promise in the sense of something that may be accepted or not; it is instead a factual event that has already taken place in the constitution of every human being. For this reason the possibility of God's communication of Himself represents, for human beings, not simply some utopia or distant goal that believers, cognizant of their radical dependency, hope for but can only aim at asymptotically. Rather it reaches its absolute high point and its cosmic, irreversible reality in the concreteness of history. The event of God becoming a human being, the incarnation of the *Logos*, stands for all of this. Accordingly, given the sense of the Christological point of departure of Karl Rahner's theology, it is correct and evident that Christology is to be labeled the "beginning and end of anthropology."[55]

In Jesus Christ, God's decisive promise and offer of Himself to human beings is realized and mediated in its historically concrete objectification. For this reason, from both divine and human standpoints, Christology appears as the most radical foundation and elevation of an anthropological theology. Theology and anthropology reveal their ultimate ground and meaning in the hypostatic union of the God-Man, Jesus Christ. "If God Himself is a human being and remains one for all eternity, if because of this all theology remains for all eternity anthropology, if the human being is prevented from thinking little of itself (since then it would, indeed, think little of God), then the human being is for all eternity the spoken mystery of God that shares for all eternity in the mystery of its ground."[56]

The Conception of a "Transcendental Christology" and Its Anthropological Relevance[57]

In the form of Jesus Christ, the incarnated *Logos* of God reveals itself as the unsurpassable high point of the history of humanity. Because the divine *Logos* in this way reveals itself such that human beings encounter a final and definitive determination of their essence as beings directed to God, Rahner is convinced that the "idea of the God-Man" requires in the subject who grasps it a transcendentally anthropological horizon. Within this horizon it is possible to thematize precisely the way in which this subject, the human being, is referred to and dependent upon the experience of an "absolute savior." In other words, if the radical contingency and questionableness of human existence first finds its ultimate, constitutive answer in the promise of Christ, then precisely from an anthropological viewpoint "a transcendental Christology, one that inquires into the a priori possibilities in the human being for the coming of the message of Christ, is explicitly necessary."[58]

A transcendental Christology of this sort is to be understood first as "Christology from below,"[59] because, taking the human being and its understanding of itself as the point of departure, it searches for an understanding of God's becoming a human being. It is thereby at the same time a "Christology searching for answers," precisely insofar as the question of salvation as an anthropologically unavoidable question already puts the human being in a position of having to search for the "absolute savior," that is to say, for the one human being in whom the human being's most pressing question and God's promise have become one.

For this reason it is necessary to translate an "ontic Christology" into an "ontological Christology."[60] With full recognition of the abiding validity of the Christological dogmas of Chalcedon, Rahner views this translation as having the great advantage that, "already from the outset and in its first conceptual steps, it grasps the 'nature' that takes on divinity not as some thing-like matter but rather as transcendental spirituality."[61]

The concept of this "transcendental Christology" naturally cannot be constructed as some rationalistic, ahistorical deduction of the "idea" of the God-Man as an "absolute savior," that is to say, a deduction that, quite independently of the historically concrete appearance of Jesus Christ as the God-Man, would assume the incarnation of the *Logos* solely as the necessary epitomization of some abstract, constantly self-surpassing evolutional movement of the human spirit.[62] To the contrary! The transcendental deduction of the idea "is always the historically subsequent reflection on a concrete experience, a reflection that explicitly sees the 'necessary' in the factual."[63]

In this theological project, Christology is the fulfillment of anthropology, the fulfillment, to be sure, within the possibilities of anthropology, though not simply in its "logical" consequences. In its innermost essence, God's becoming a human being remains a matter of grace, not some datum that can be expected anthropologically. For this reason as well, the Christological dimension first discloses itself on the basis of an event that has factually and historically come to be, the arrival of the divine *Logos* in Jesus Christ.

In Rahner's conception of the matter, the dimensions of anthropology retain their essential form and dynamic in the event of Christ. As K. P. Fischer, summing things up, puts it, "God's descent" signifies "the human being's ascent,"[64] and because of this, Christology can legitimately be said to be "anthropology in a process of transcending itself," and anthropology in turn can be legitimately considered "deficient Christology."[65] For this reason, the theological relevance of Christology for anthropology discloses itself in the fundamental determination: "Christ as the 'Ek-sistence' of the human being."[66]

The Incarnation as the Epitome of the Encounter between God and Human Beings

"The Word of God has become a human being." This fundamental assertion of Christology explicates the irrevocable elementary unity between divine and human nature, a unity posited in an absolute way in the person of Jesus Christ, in the offer and acceptance of God's communication of Himself to humanity. Not only posited, this unity "is here" [*ist da*] in an irreversible way. For the Incarnation in its essence signals not simply a regional or peripheral reality in the relation of God to human beings, but rather signifies the very epitome of it; that is to say, it is not only posited by God, but rather is God *Himself*. "If the offer itself, however, is a human reality as an absolute gift of grace, and should this offer really be absolutely that of God, then it is the absolute reality for God; hence, precisely what we call, properly understood, *unio hypostatica*."[67]

If the *Logos* becomes a human being, then that cannot mean merely the assumption of a reality which would have no internal relation to the one taking on that reality or which could just as well be replaced by something else. Rather God takes on human nature as His own and thereby gives it its meaning and its direction. God's becoming a human being, the Incarnation, thus signals the "uniquely supreme instance of someone fully realizing the essence of human reality, by virtue of the fact that this human being, because He gives Himself away, yielding to the absolute mystery, is what we call 'God.' "[68] The radical possibility of God's self-externalization thus grounds the possibility of the existence of the human being. The human being is, thereby, in the original definition, the "*potentia oboedientialis* for the hypostatic union"[69] or, expressed in a different way, "the possible being-other of the self-externalization of God and the possible brother of Christ."[70] With this, an elementary unity is established between the historical, finite question that the human being is and the infinite, eternal answer that God is.

The hypostatic union of the event of Christ thus figures in Karl Rahner's argumentation as the central dimension for the identification of the legitimacy of the anthropological turn in theology. It ultimately provides the founding criterion of the synthetic unity among anthropology, Christology, and theology. By reason of the fact that it "is the union of the authentic essence of God and of the human being in the personal self-assertion of God in His eternal *Logos*, Christology is the beginning and the end of anthropology and this anthropology, in the most radical realization of it, is for all eternity theology."[71]

Within the framework of this systematic consideration, theology's anthropological point of departure is grounded with unavoidable necessity in Christology and reaches its high point in the demand "to encounter God in the human being and ultimately, in the human being in whom God finally is present in the world and historically appears, in Jesus Christus."[72]

Overview: The Anthropologically Mediated Content of Theological Themes

Whenever theology is pursued with scientific rigor and in an "intellectually honest" manner, it does not fail to reflect on the basic anthropological constants of the human essence and the way in which the latter is conditioned, without negating itself, its method and its content, and leading to absurdity. The material content of the anthropological "objects" or "themes" constantly steers theological thinking back to the human being as "the entity that is referred to God and must understand itself from the divine standpoint and on the basis of it."[73]

In Karl Rahner's conception of theology, the essential, anthropological dimension of every theological question reveals itself in the reciprocity and constitutive *unity of the experience of God and the experience of oneself.* Wherever a human being radically and comprehensively realizes its essence as a person and subject in all its experiences, the transcendent ground of this essence reveals itself at the same time therein. This transcendent ground reveals itself as the "holy mystery," turning the human being back to the constitutive horizon of its transcendental referredness. Thus the experience of the self remains the place and the condition for the experience of God and vice versa.

Within the theological-anthropological relation of nature and grace, in his conception of the "supernatural existential," Rahner procures the integral center of gravity for theology, a theology with an anthropological point of departure. The meaning of that supernatural existential is elaborated as follows. "It is, however, not possible to speak meaningfully of this grace at all other than in a transcendental-anthropological investigation. For, without detracting from the fact that this grace is God Himself in self-mediation, it is no 'thing,' but rather a determination of the spiritual subject as such to be the immediacy to God."[74]

Accordingly, as far as its anthropological implications are concerned, God's gracious communication of Himself can be formulated as "a modification of our transcendentality as such, radicalizing it to the limit."[75] This way of determining the relation finds its unifying ground and at the same time its normative standard in the reality of the event of Christ, if one reflects therein on the *anthropological consequences* of the hypostatic union. "What the Incarnation is, is only rightly understood when the humanity of Christ is not only the instrument, something ultimately still external, by means of which a God that remains invisible speaks, but rather precisely what God Himself (remaining God) becomes, when he externalizes Himself in the dimension of the other-than-Himself, the dimension of what is not divine."[76] To be a human being means then originally "*potentia oboedientalis* for the hypostatic union and for the grace (Christi)."[77]

Viewed in this way, human "nature" has the ground of its possibility in the reality of the "supernature," and it is first in its theological foundation that it really comes to itself, revealing therein its authentic mystery: "The human being is the event of the absolute self-communication of God."[78]

For the relation of divine and human reality to one another and thus for any theology beginning by way of anthropology, this means ultimately and fundamentally that "the most objective thing about the reality of salvation, namely, God and His grace, appears at the same time as the most subjective thing about human beings, namely, the spiritual subject's immediacy to God by virtue of this subject itself."[79]

NOTES

1. K. H. Weger, *Karl Rahner. Eine Einführung in sein theologisches Denken*, 40.

2. K. Rahner, "Die theologische Dimension der Frage nach dem Menschen," *Schriften zur Theologie* 12 (1975): 390.

3. Ibid. See K. Rahner, "Anthropozentrik," *Lexikon für Theologie und Kirche*, 2nd ed., vol. 1 (Freiburg: Herder, 1957), 632–34.

4. Cf. the essay by Rahner with this title: "Selbsterfahrung und Gotteserfahrung," *Schriften zur Theologie* 10(1972): 133–44.

5. K. Rahner, *Grundkurs*, 40 (29).

6. K. Rahner, "Selbsterfahrung und Gotteserfahrung," 136.

7. Ibid.

8. A prime example of what has been named "transcendental analysis of the experience of existence" may be found in the first two "paths" of the *Foundations of Christian Faith* (*Grundkurs*, 35–96 [24–89]). Rahner had already devoted his early philosophical works, so foundational for his entire creative effort, to this plan; see K. Rahner, *Geist in Welt* (*Spirit in the World*) and *Hörer des Wortes* (*Hearers of the Word*). The analysis of the basic human processes and accomplishments, undertaken in the *Foundations of Christian Faith*, presents a kind of final review and endpoint in the history of the author's thinking and thus provides the foundation for the presentation attempted in what follows.

9. Rahner, *Grundkurs*, 37 (26).

10. K. Raffelt and K. Rahner, "Anthropologie und Theologie," in *Christlicher Glaube in moderner Gesellschaft*, ed. F. Böckle et al., vol. 24. (Freiburg: Herder, 1981), 16.

11. K. Rahner, *Grundkurs*, 62 (52).

12. K. Rahner, *Grundkurs*, 41 (30). While Rahner takes the trouble to point out the human being's transcendental experience of the subject by means of key examples, precisely in the basic ways that knowledge and freedom are carried out, K. H. Weger refers to the fact that the concentration on these two basic ways that human existence is realized by no means has an exclusive character, but rather that this experience "is always and unavoidably given in each conscious, mental act along with it as the condition of its possibility" (K. H. Weger, *Karl Rahner: Eine Einführung in sein theologisches Denken*, 51). In another passage Rahner himself identifies further places of such a transcendental experience including, among others, loneliness, personal love, responsibility, death, joy, anxiety, guilt; "thus one

should and one must proceed further in order to suggest the single, primordial experience of the human being in a thousand declinations." See K. Rahner, "Gotteserfahrung heute," *Schriften zur Theologie* 9 (1970): 168.

13. K. Rahner, *Grundkurs*, 41 (30).
14. K. Raffelt and K. Rahner, "Anthropologie und Theologie," 14.
15. On the philosophical concept of the person and the subject in general, see the overview by A. Halder, "Anthropologie. I. Philosophische Anthropologie," *Staatslexikon*, 7th ed. (Freiburg: Herder, 1985), 1: 169ff and "Person. I. Begriffsgeschichte," *Lexikon für Theologie und Kirche*, 2nd ed., 8: 289ff.
16. K. Rahner, *Grundkurs*, 42–43 (32).
17. Ibid., 45 (35).
18. K. Rahner, "Anthropologie. Theologische Anthropologie," *Sacramentum Mundi* (Freiburg: Herder, 1967): 180.
19. K. Rahner, *Grundkurs*, 45 (34).
20. An impressive, synthetic view of the basic principles of these two "early works" of Rahner is presented by K. P. Fischer in *Der Mensch als Geheimnis. Die Anthropologie Karl Rahners*, 83–205. In the second part of the study the attempt is made to synthesize the linking, basic thought under the title "Hearer of the Word as Spirit in the World." P. Eicher, by contrast, gives an interpretation with an explicitly philosophical orientation, an interpretation of human spirituality as the criterion for the ontological constitution of the human essence which thereby necessarily misses the basic intention of Rahner, sketched above. See P. Eicher, *Die anthropologische Wende*, 257–324.
21. K. Rahner, *Hörer des Wortes*, 73.
22. Ibid., 85.
23. Ibid., 86.
24. Ibid., 85.
25. Ibid., 77.
26. K. Rahner, *Grundkurs*, 44 (33).
27. Ibid., 46 (35).
28. K. H. Weger, *Karl Rahner. Eine Einführung in sein theologisches Denken*, 64.
29. K. Rahner, *Grundkurs*, 74 (65–66).
30. K. Rahner, "Über den Begriff des Geheimnisses in der katholischen Theologie," *Schriften zur Theologie* 4 (1960): 73.

31. K. Rahner, *Grundkurs*, 32 (21).
32. See K. P. Fischer, *Der Mensch als Geheimnis: Die Anthropologie Karl Rahners*, 192. In addition to Rahner's lectures on the concept of the mystery—see K. Rahner, "Über den Begriff des Geheimnisses in der katholischen Theologie," *Schriften zur Theologie* 4 (1960): 51–99—Fischer appeals here chiefly to a transcript of a tape recording of the seminar entitled "The Mystery" conducted by K. Rahner in 1957/58. In regard to these reflections oriented towards the concept of the mystery in Karl Rahner's theology as well as other well-drawn points, see H. Vorgrimler (ed.), *Wagnis Theologie: Erfahrungen mit der Theologie Karl Rahners*, 13.
33. K. P. Fischer, *Der Mensch als Geheimnis: Die Anthropologie Karl Rahners*, 44.
34. K. Rahner, "Über den Begriff des Geheimnisses in der katholischen Theologie," *Schriften zur Theologie* 4 (1960): 60.
35. See K. Rahner, "Überlegungen zur Methode der Theologie," *Schriften zur Theologie* 9 (1970): 79–126, esp. pp. 113–26.
36. For an extensive discussion of this matter, see K. Rahner, "Über den Begriff des Geheimnisses in der katholischen Theologie," *Schriften zur Theologie* 4 (1960), especially the introductory deliberations to the second lecture (67–69). On the speculative question about the extent to which God Himself can be an "incomprehensible" mystery, see K. P. Fischer's discussion of the question "Is God Himself a mystery?" in his *Der Mensch als Geheimnis: Die Anthropologie Karl Rahners*, 189–93.
37. K. Lehmann, "In memoriam Karl Rahner," Tribute on Bavarian Radio: "Catholic World" on April 1, 1984, 8:00–8:30 (Bavarian Radio: Telescript from April 1, 1986, 5).
38. K. H. Weger, *Karl Rahner: Eine Einführung in sein theologisches Denken*, 79.
39. " 'Gnade als Mitte menschlicher Existenz.' Interview with Karl Rahner," *Herder Korrespondenz* 28 (1974): 83.
40. K. Rahner, "Theologie und Anthropologie," *Schriften zur Theologie* 8 (1967): 53.
41. Ibid., 60.
42. K. Rahner, *Grundkurs*, 134 (128).
43. Ibid., 135 (129).
44. See K. Rahner, *Grundkurs*, 127f (121).
45. Ibid., 126 (120).
46. Ibid., 128 (122).

47. Ibid., 125 (119) and elsewhere.
48. On this matter see above in Chapter 2, Section I: "The Experience of the Self and the Experience of God."
49. K. Rahner, "Die theologische Dimension der Frage nach dem Menschen," *Schriften zur Theologie* 12 (1975): 400f.
50. K. Rahner, *Grundkurs*, 135 (132).
51. K. Rahner, "Anthropologie. Theologische Anthropologie," *Sacramentum Mundi* (Freiburg: Herder, 1967), 1: 182.
52. K. Rahner, "Theologie und Anthropologie," *Schriften zur Theologie* 8 (1967): 54.
53. Ibid.
54. K. Rahner, "Mensch: Zum theologischen Begriff des Menschen," *Sacramentum Mundi* (Freiburg: Herder, 1969), 3: 416.
55. I. Bokwa, *Christologie als Anfang und Ende der Anthropologie: Über das gegenseitige Verhältnis zwischen Christologie und Anthropologie bei Karl Rahner* (Frankfurt and New York: Peter Lang, 1990).
56. K. Rahner, *Grundkurs*, 223 (225).
57. In this connection the concern is not to provide an explicit presentation of Karl Rahner's Christological project. For this, see in particular K. Rahner and W. Thysing, *Christologie— systematisch und exegetisch: Grundlinien einer systematischen Christologie* (Freiburg: Herder, 1972). Also noteworthy is the quite extensive "sixth sequence" of the *Foundation of Christian Faith* on Jesus Christ (K. Rahner, *Grundkurs*, 178–312 [176–321]) as a synthetic and compendious treatment of this theme. Rahner's existentializing talent shows itself, of course, at best in the "Theological Meditation"; see K. Rahner, *Ich glaube an Jesus Christus* (Einsiedeln: Benziger, 1968). In contrast to the latter, the particular focus that is supposed to be obtained here is the anthropological relevance of this Christological point of departure of Rahner.
58. K. Rahner, *Grundkurs*, 207 (207).
59. See K. H. Ohlig, "Impulse zu einer 'Christologie von unten' bei Karl Rahner," *Wagnis Theologie: Erfahrungen mit der Theologie Karl Rahners*, 259–73. In order to ward off various misunderstandings of the concept "from below," it should be emphasized that it signifies no social revolutionary or political reality, but rather merely a philosophical-methodical reality.
60. K. Rahner, "Theologie und Anthropologie," *Schriften zur Theologie* 8 (1967): 54.

61. Ibid. On the same page Karl Rahner elucidates this "anthropological-ontological translation" of the event of Christ in the following way: "Since here essence and being are (and do not merely 'have') self-givenness and transcendence, it must be possible in a fundamental way to articulate the substantial unity with the *Logos* in the conceptual structure of self-givenness and transcendence and to translate the unity into that structure so that what the 'hypostatic union' says is really clear enough and adequately protected from a mythological misunderstanding."

62. Rahner here makes reference to a "Christology of the *Logos*," as it is exemplarily projected in Teilhard de Chardin's evolutional view of the world. That Rahner does not occupy a position utterly removed from this sort of interpretation is shown by the extensive first chapter of his Christology in the *Foundations of Christian Faith*, which is entitled "Christology within an Evolutional World-View"; see K. Rahner, *Grundkurs*, 180–202. Regarding the theological problem surrounding Teilhard de Chardin, see Th. Brock, *Das Problem der Freiheit im Werk von Pierre Teilhard de Chardin* (Mainz: Matthius-Grunewald, 1977), 435–530; S. M. Daecke, "Das Ja und das Nein des Konzils zu Teilhard," in *Die Autorität der Freiheit: Gegenwart des Konzils und Zukunft der Kirche im ökumenischen Disput*, vol. 3, ed. J. Ch. Hampe (Munich: Kösel, 1967), 98–112; W. Klein, *Teilhard de Chardin und das zweite Vatikanische Konzil: Ein Vergleich der Pastoralkonstitution über die Kirche in der Welt von heute mit Aspekten der Weltschau Pierre Teilhards de Chardin*, Abhandlungen zur Sozialethik, vol. 8 (Munich: F. Schönigh, 1979); O. Spülbeck, "Teilhard de Chardin und die Pastoralkonstitution," in *Die Autorität der Freiheit*, vol. 3, 86–97.

63. K. Rahner, "Transzendentaltheologie," *Sacramentum Mundi* (Freiburg: Herder, 1960), 4: 990.

64. K. P. Fischer, *Der Mensch als Geheimnis:. Die Anthropologie Karl Rahners*, 293.

65. Ibid.

66. Ibid., 302.

67. K. Rahner, *Grundkurs*, 202 (202).

68. Ibid., 216 (218).

69. Ibid.

70. K. Rahner, "Anthropologie. Theologische Anthropologie," *Sacramentum Mundi* (Freiburg: Herder, 1967), 1: 185.

71. K. Rahner, *Grundkurs*, 223 (225).
72. K. Rahner, "Transzendentaltheologie," *Sacramentum Mundi* (Freiburg: Herder, 1969), 4: 992.
73. K. Rahner, "Mensch: Zum theologischen Begriff des Menschen," *Sacramentum Mundi* (Freiburg: Herder, 1969), 3: 411.
74. K. Rahner, "Theologie und Anthropologie," *Schriften zur Theologie* 8 (1967): 53.
75. K. Rahner, *Grundkurs*, 138 (132).
76. K. Rahner, "Grundsätzliche Überlegungen zur Anthropologie und Protologie im Rahmen der Theologie," *Mysterium Salutis* (Einsiedeln: Benziger, 1967), 2: 416.
77. K. Rahner, "Anthropologie. Theologische Anthropologie," 185.
78. K. Rahner, *Grundkurs*, 125 (119). Here a central axiom of the Rahnerian point of departure is already revealed. The supernatural is never determined in some radically inductive sense from the standpoint of the natural, but rather just the reverse. Nature is as such always a "deficient mode" of the supernatural and it is first communicated to itself in the "supernatural act" of radicalization through grace.
79. K. Lehmann, "Karl Rahner. Ein Porträt," in K. Lehmann and A. Raffelt, eds., *Rechenschaft des Glaubens: Karl Rahner—Lesebuch*, 37*.

3

The Formal–Methodological Method of the Starting Point: Theology as Transcendental Reflection

"TRANSCENDENTAL ANTHROPOLOGY is a correct characterization of my theology," Karl Rahner reaffirms in an interview in the *Herder Korrespondenz* on the occasion of his seventieth birthday, thereby giving pointed conceptual expression to the two basic contours of his theological thinking.[1] Along with the composition of its content which has theology beginning materially as anthropology in a necessary recourse to human nature, the manner of its execution consists methodologically in transcendental reflection; hence, it may be characterized formally as *transcendental theology*.

The concept of transcendental theology employed in theology today (which the *Lexikon für Theologie und Kirche*, even in its second edition, still does not recognize) essentially goes back to the work of Karl Rahner. The most essential features of the notion were coined by him. By "transcendental theology" he understands "the systematic theology which (a) makes use of the tools of a transcendental philosophy, and also (b) thematizes the a priori conditions in the believing subject for the knowledge of important truths of the faith, doing so on the basis of genuine theological inquiries and much more explicitly than in the past where these conditions were thematized only in a quite general sense."[2]

According to Immanuel Kant's famous philosophical definition, transcendental knowledge requires that for every realm of objects, in addition to the investigation of those objects themselves, an inquiry also be made into the constitutive conditions of the possibility of knowledge of these objects, as those conditions present themselves in the knowing subject.[3] For Rahner, who leans on this definition, it follows from the application of its basic insight to theology "that, precisely in the case of each dogmatic object, one also inquire into the necessary conditions in the theological subject for knowing that object, demonstrate that there are such a priori conditions for the knowledge of this object, and show that they themselves already imply and express something about the object as well as the manner, method, and limits of knowing it."[4]

If in this way the human being is conceived as the "transcendental subject" of theology and, with that, the human being's constitutive role for every theological theme is appreciated, then it becomes readily apparent that the transcendental reflection, that is to say, the formal, methodological aspect of this theology, also implies that human beings form an essential part of its genuine point of departure.

Nevertheless, it is not to be forgotten in this regard that, in contrast to the demonstration of the fundamental possibility and necessity of an anthropological turn in theology, the way adopted by Rahner to carry out this turn—the transcendental theological method—is motivated and fashioned not in the first place by theology, but rather, as is easily shown, by philosophy. Rahner is, to be sure, convinced that this way also makes itself evident on the basis of revelation and that it derives its profoundest justification precisely from the intersection, founded on human nature, of subjectivity and objectivity in theological knowledge. Nonetheless, because of the extensive philosophical character of its origins, there is a far higher contingency to this methodological aspect of his thinking than there is to its content. In another epoch within the history of thought, that is to say, in the face of underlying cultural and philosophical conditions that were altered or fundamentally transformed, this methodological aspect might well have turned out quite differently.

A methodological problem arises for Rahner from the fact that the determination of the relation between the concepts of transcendental theology and transcendental philosophy is, in part, not clarified.[5] He understands transcendental theology in analogy with the concept of transcendental philosophy as the consistent and requisite application of transcendental philosophy to theological themes. "Transcendental theology is theology which makes use of transcendental philosophy as a method."[6] By way of grounding this claim, Rahner adds: "By this not only a verbal analogy is suggested. As far as the matter at hand is concerned, transcendental philosophy and transcendental theology have to do with one another and cannot be separated from one another at all."[7]

In such an affirmative determination of the relation, there is, in the first place, an acceptance of the fact that fundamentally, as far as the history of thought is concerned, the origin of the transcendental idea is the philosophical tradition. At the same time a constructive connection to theology is set up, a connection which necessarily and quite evidently not only influences its way of proceeding methodologically, but also acquires an immediately material relevance in regard to its content. This observation pays tribute to Hegel's fundamental insight, namely, "that the application of an instrument to some matter . . . does not leave it as it is, but rather also forms and alters it."[8] So understood, the transcendental method together with the philosophical implications belonging to it becomes a constitutive principle of theology itself. "Since philosophy is not only an instrument for theology, approaching the latter as it were from the outside, but rather a factor internal to theology itself, the preliminary determination of transcendental theology that has just been made on the basis of transcendental philosophy does not signify an alienation of theology."[9]

Yet, in contrast to this innocently integrational concept of the coordination of philosophy and theology, Rahner also determines their relation in a way that is limited, as far as the content is concerned, and theologically modified. Representative of this more restricted view is Rahner's assertion that "the point of departure of a transcendental theology is genuinely theological."[10]

If Rahner at first still insisted on an inseparability of transcendental philosophy and transcendental theology as far as the subject matter of the disciplines and the history of thought are concerned, he later does away with this relation in favor of theology. If in the course of establishing the idea of a transcendental theology "recourse is had to a transcendental philosophy, it does not," he maintains, "take its genuinely theological character from the latter for the following reason: the theological consideration of the 'nature' of the human being as a condition of the possibility of grace belongs to theology itself and thus is theology which looks like philosophy."[11]

In Rahner's view, there is an obvious rationale for giving a genuinely theological determination of the human being as a transcendental subject. Precisely when a human being reflects on the unity and totality of his or her nature, what is always in question alongside and even prior to all other ultimate, philosophical determinations of his or her existence is the theological state of being, a state of being referred, in the final analysis, to something higher, the question of his or her salvation. "To understand the reality of salvation in this way means, however, nothing other than grasping it transcendentally, that is to say, in relation to the transcendental subject that is such 'by nature' and precisely so constituted is radicalized by what we call 'grace.' "[12] Hence, to pursue transcendental philosophy means ultimately nothing other than to be implicitly pursuing theology when, thereby, the graced constitution of the transcendental subject is properly realized and adequately established and expressed in its relevance for the transcendental experience of the human being.

"In our historical situation, a philosophy absolutely free of theology is not possible at all," Rahner affirms by way of summarizing his viewpoint, arriving thereby at a novel, metaphilosophically oriented determination of the relation between transcendental philosophy and transcendental theology.[13]

On the one hand, the methodological relation and even the historical priority of transcendental philosophy to transcendental theology, at least in regard to the former's conceptual-reflexive equipment, is thoroughly recognized. On the other hand, however, Rahner's stated intention remains that of setting up the transcendental inquiry on the basis of the essence of theology itself. According to Rahner, this claim is justified by the fact that every theoretical reflection and self-interpretation of human existence—thus, philosophy—always sees itself confronted from the outset with the historical fact signifying faith, revelation and grace. For this reason alone, philosophy cannot take its point of departure from anything that lies outside the genuinely theological horizon of inquiry in the believing subject without negating essential elements in the human being's experience of himself and abbreviating the complexity of human existence. The transcendental subject's existential experience of totality must, however, remain in the middle of things if one intends to pursue theology as transcendental theology. L. B. Puntel, who worked with Karl Rahner for many years, characterizes in the following way this basic feature of the theology of experience in the transcendental theological thinking of his teacher: "The guiding principle of Rahner's entire theology is born and determined by the insight that every (philosophical and) theological truth can and, even more so, must be understood, elaborated, and recognized as meaningful or even ineluctable, only if it is obtained from the analysis of a human action [*Vollzug*]. On this insight rests Rahner's insistence on the indissoluble unity of theological truth and life or, better, something carried out in an existential way."[14]

Bound up with this manner of methodically beginning with the "existential action" of human existence is the fundamental determinacy of the transcendental theological inquiry (a determinacy that belongs to the theology of experience). On the one hand, that point of departure and that fundamental determinacy together bring with them an unavoidable subjectivity in theology, a subjectivity that the opponents of an anthropologically oriented theology would like to eliminate in the name of "objective sacred facts." On the other hand and in view of the historically contingent character of the revelation, the problem presents itself of how the a priori necessary structures of the epistemological subject can be mediated with the underivable a posteriori experience of history or, in other words, how transcendentality and categoriality can be reconciled.

THE TURN TO THE SUBJECT

According to Rahner, "the interpretation of the entirety of dogmatic theology as transcendental anthropology [contains] the requirement that every dogmatic theme be considered also in terms of its transcendental side and that, for this reason, one must pose to oneself the question of what sort of material content is already contained in the a priori 'structures' of the theological subject itself, implicitly co-expressed in the respective theological assertion."[15] In this regard Christian revelation is, for two distinct reasons, a truth that is subjective and refers to a subject. In the first place, the truth of Christian revelation is always concerned with a totality that never simply comes to us merely in the form of a thing or as some objective and objectifiable "theme of belief." In the second place what is at stake in Christian revelation is not some "theoretical" truth as a doctrine, but rather, as far as its profoundest intention is concerned, "existential" truth, a truth that is first adequately and really perceived when it is understood as an appeal, not only to knowledge, but also to human freedom.

From the first of these two points it follows that a theology setting out from a transcendentally anthropological point of view is required to pursue theology as a transcendental reflection and therein—in recognition of the ineliminable intersection of an objective and a subjective side to knowledge in every case—to articulate human cognizing subjectivity as an existential and transcendental totality. From the latter of the two points made in the previous paragraph, the necessity emerges of making sure that a barrier is no longer set up between theoretical and practical reason, between knowing and acting.[16]

The Intersection of Subjectivity and Objectivity in Knowledge

The intersection of subjectivity and objectivity in transcendental knowledge is a doctrine classically developed by Kant.[17] In analogous application of the same basic doctrine, Rahner also clings to this relation of reciprocal conditioning. "Knowledge does not bring only the known, but also the knower into play; that is to say, it is dependent not only on the peculiarities of the object, but rather also on the essential structure of the subject who knows. The relation of reciprocal conditioning between the knowing subject and the known object as known and knowable is the object of a transcendental inquiry."[18]

In the course of one's preoccupation and transactions with the individual objects that make up the reality of categorial experience, an explicit reflection upon the conditions of the possibility of knowing them can be left undone. But while such reflection can be omitted in those cases, it is absolutely impermissible in the realm of theological knowledge. For it is precisely the distinguishing feature of every theological question that therein the person questioning and what is being questioned present more than merely objectifiable individual realities. "Not only is [the inquiring human being] as a subject also inquired into, because it is a 'material' piece of this whole, but rather it must be inquired into since the whole (as the horizon of transcendentality) is and can only be given in the subject as such on the basis of its own subjective, distinctive manner."[19] But God, too, as the aimed-for, formal object of this inquiry is "no object alongside others in the a posteriori realm of experience, but rather the original ground and the absolute future of all reality."[20] Theology is for that reason—as transcendental reflection—always reflection on the whole of reality.

Because the whole as such does not explicitly come forth in the realm of a posteriori experience, in the world of categorial objects, Kant drew the conclusion that metaphysical knowledge is impossible. For theoretical reasons, the existence of God is not to be proven, but neither is its possibility to be denied; on the basis of ethics, however, God could be introduced as a "postulate of practical reason." In contrast to Kant's approach, Karl Rahner latches on to the work of J. Maréchal and proceeds down another path. By means of the unthematic transcendental experience of the whole and what is all-encompassing, the epistemological subject is already "supernaturally finalized" towards the transcendental ground of its essence. That means "that—without detracting from all the mediatedness of this self-possession through the spatial-temporal experience of sensuously given objects—this subject is in a fundamental sense and of itself the pure openness for absolutely everything, for being in general."[21] Since, however, the experience of the infinite can neither stem from the categorially experienceable external world of objects, nor have its origin in the finitude of the subject itself, this unavoidable experience of transcendence on the part of the subject must be understood as a real reference to an objectively existing, holistic reality named 'God.' For this reason, Rahner affirms categorially: "The knowing subject's knowledge of its very self is always also a knowledge of metaphysical (in an objective sense 'transcendental') structures of the object itself."[22]

In this way, within the framework of transcendental reflection, one passes from subjectivity over into objectivity. Transcendental anthropology thus breaks through its epistemological confinement into the realm of the transcendent. "The transcendental experience is the experience of transcendence, an experience in which the structure of the subject and thereby also the ultimate structure of all conceivable objects of knowledge are given in a single reality and in identity."[23]

This decisive distinction between Kant's understanding of transcendental philosophy and Rahner's point of departure may be construed and criticized as an illegitimate extension of the transcendental method to a ground no longer capable of supporting it,[24] or it may be applauded as a necessary and indispensable enriching of a system that is too rigoristically confined to knowledge of what is empirically objective. This ultimately idle debate notwithstanding, the fruitfulness of such an expanded transcendental condition lies for Rahner in its application to theological objects or themes. The methodological handiness of this point of departure reveals itself precisely in the confrontation of the knowing subject's transcendentally and a priori formed structure with the objects of theology which rest upon a posteriori revelation. A word of God can at bottom only be really understood and recognized as such in the context of a transcendental reflection. "It must be soberly seen that there is no word of God that does not make its appearance from the outset as something that is not suited to belief, that is to say, that does not imply all those epistemological problems consisting in the fact that the 'in itself' of a known reality must be given in a subjective act and, hence, the subjectivity of the one who knows is to be established in such a way that, for the peculiarity of its 'object,' it opens up the possibility for the latter to show itself."[25] Because of this, it is a valid requirement of any theology of revelation that what it is must become clear to it in transcendental reflection on the character internal to it and, at the same time, on the condition of its possibility, namely, that transcendentally unrestricted horizon of the human spirit on the basis of which something like a word of God can first be understood. " 'Natural-philosophical' theology is, first and last, not an occupation alongside a theology of revelation such that both could be pursued in complete independence of one another, but rather a character internal to the theology of revelation itself."[26]

The Transcendental Unity of Knowledge and Freedom

Whereas Kant, in establishing transcendental philosophy, had drawn a clear line of demarcation between theoretical and practical reason, between knowledge and freedom, both realms fall together into a unity for Rahner as constituents of the theological subject in the transcendental experience. "This transcendental experience is naturally not merely an experience of pure cognition as such, but rather also of willing and of freedom, to which the same character of transcendentality applies; hence, it is always possible to inquire in a fundamental way into the 'towards which' and 'from which' [*Woraufhin und Wovonher*] of the subject as at once both a knower and a free agent."[27]

Hence, where the human being experiences himself as a subject, the ground of the roots of human freedom is at the same time posited, and in an original sense, responsibility and freedom are experienced at the core of one's own existence. "Insofar as the human being is the essence of transcendence, he is also confronted with himself, handed over to himself, and thus a person and subject. For only there, where the infinity of being—unveiling itself and withdrawing—prevails, does an entity have a place and standpoint on the basis of which he can take over what it means for him to be himself."[28]

If the place of human freedom is thus rooted in the human essence constituted by the experience of transcendence, and if a human being first experiences himself (or herself, as the case may be) on the basis of this experience of transcendence in his grandeur and finitude as a transcendental subject, then he is therein at one and the same time handed over to himself in responsibility and yet always also withdrawn from himself. Thus he can never adequately retrieve and thematize his transcendental experience, since it pulls back from conceptual knowledge in accordance with its unthematic nature, a nature grounded in the experience of transcendence. It can only be perceived when it is admitted and taken up in lived freedom. Rahner is convinced that this transcendental experience of the human essence is accordingly grounded in that personal depth of the subject, in which knowledge and the act of freedom are no longer to be separated.[29]

For the theological knowledge that is specified as transcendental reflection signifies this: It can never be "compelling" in a categorially-objective sense, for it is always *knowledge in freedom*. As a logical consequence of this, the following holds for all knowledge of God and analogously for the entire self-understanding of theology as science: "The concept 'God' is not a comprehending of God through which the human being becomes master of the mystery, but rather a matter of letting-oneself-be-comprehended by a mystery that makes itself present and always withdraws itself."[30]

Objectivity in Subjectivity

If theology—in Rahner's sense—is pursued as a transcendental reflection that of necessity takes anthropology as its point of departure, it is unavoidably referred to subjectivity, indeed, committed to the latter and the structures in theological knowledge that are given with that subjectivity. In the eyes of opponents of an "anthropological turn," however, this move exposes such a theology to the reproach of falling prey to an arbitrary relativism in which the "objective" validity of the "sacred facts" could no longer be sustained.

Rahner intends to overturn this aporia by according an objective significance to the subjective components in the transcendental process of knowledge. "A transcendental inquiry is thus not simply a question in addition to the question of the object that originally and in an a posteriori-empirical manner appears before us, but rather in the transcendental question the knowledge of the original object itself first comes to the fullness of what it essentially is."[31] In this sense, as already shown above, the subject's transcendental knowledge also contains essential features of the object itself from the outset. It is always "a knowledge of metaphysical (in an objective sense, 'transcendental') structures of the object itself."[32]

Hence, precisely in view of the specific character of theological assertions, Rahner's intention of establishing objective truth in the subjective, transcendental manner of knowing moves between two dubious extremes. On the one hand, there is the constant threat of a latent "danger of idealism," constantly criticized in modern philosophy, a danger the ultimate consequence of which signifies the identification of subject and object and, thereby, the dissolution of anything like an objective character at all. On the other hand, as far as any sort of metaphysical knowledge is concerned, it is commonplace today to maintain an agnosticism based upon Kant's "critique of theoretical reason," such that assertions about being are discarded as claims involving "no real predicate." The reality of complex concepts of reason such as those of the soul, the world, and God have been referred to the foundational realm belonging to practical reason.

Rahner's solution to this aporia starts out in nuanced fashion. "God in Himself" and "God for us" do not in principle present alternatives if they are considered solely at the level of that transcendental experience. At that level, "the human being is in possession of himself and radically withdrawn from himself, since the mystery as something absolute both promises itself to him and holds the human being at a distance from itself, distinguishing itself from him."[33] If the content of this original experience is thematized and brought to a conceptual level, then it means that "the concept in its original basis and the reality which as such is meant by this concept merge into one or are hidden in one reality."[34]

What ultimately matters, then, is an experience which at the same time has a subjective *and* an objective character, an experience that is expressed in the following dialectical, twofold assertion: "God is the innermost reality of the finite subject and the worldly reality encountered by the latter, bearing both up from within and at the same time . . . the pervading, prevailing being in absolute, untouchable self-possession who does not disappear in the function of being the horizon of our existence."[35]

The dialectical openness of the relation of subjectivity and objectivity in theological experience is thus eminently meaningful at that profound depth where a reciprocal "immanence" of God and the human being exists, where, put theologically, God Himself offers Himself to the human being, indeed, promising to be "absolutely near" the human being. That "capacity for a genuinely dialogical relation of being 'bound' to one another up to the point of being absolutely near to one another, 'face to face,' and of 'participating in the divine nature' ultimately . . . makes the human being into an entity who, in the final analysis, is not some piece of a greater whole (world); rather, in each respectively unique manner, the whole is precisely the person, 'existence,' in contrast to what is present at hand."[36]

In Karl Rahner's view, the theological point of departure in the founding of human transcendentality, just indicated, presents an essential presupposition for the acceptability of the status of the theological mediation, the necessary synthesis between "objectivity" and "subjectivity," in the face of the criteria of classical theology. "Radical subjectivity's assertion of revelation"[37] guarantees therein that unity of subjectivity and objectivity in transcendental knowing, a unity not synthesizable on the basis of subjectively immanent categories, that must be viewed from the outset as the *conditio sine qua non* of every theology. At this level of transcendental experience, objectivity and subjectivity are conceived as *perichoresis*, as the constant dynamic motion between two poles. God Himself, for all His immanence in this relation as the goal that is aimed for and at the same time the enabling ground, does not disappear into subjectivity. In being "for us," He constantly preserves His "in Himselfness," remaining God. "The most objective character of the sacred reality is at the same time of necessity the most subjective: the immediacy of the spiritual subject to God, effected by God Himself."[38]

Transcendentality and History

If one were to construe Rahner's transcendental point of departure as amounting to a logically requisite reduction of all theology to a transcendental deduction in which historical experience and therein, in particular, the event of revelation in history would be ultimately superfluous, then one would have misunderstood him from the ground up. "For precisely the return of the subject to the transcendental conditions of the possibility of his knowledge signifies, indeed, the awareness of his undeniable referredness to history and experience, not derivable in any transcendental way."[39]

While affirming this, Rahner is well aware of the difficulties of mediating the necessary, a priori character of the transcendental subject and the contingent, a posteriori character of the object historically experienced within the relation of transcendentality and history. In the already cited interview in the *Herder Korrespondenz*, Rahner himself acknowledges: "I would say that there are few philosophical, anthropological, and theological problems that are more difficult to answer, when correctly weighed, than that of the relation of transcendentality and history."[40] Accordingly, an adequately conceived determination of this difficult relation will, on the one hand, recognize the necessary, a priori horizon of the transcendental subject as the foregoing condition of all knowledge and, on the other hand, thematize how every transcendental act of knowledge is unavoidably referred to historically categorial experience. This holds, in particular, for the determination of the place of revelation, given as an historical event, opposite the attempt at a transcendental deduction of necessary truths in a theological understanding.

The Indispensability of Historically Categorial Experience

"Transcendentality and freedom are realized in history," Rahner fundamentally affirms, thereby removing the basis for any overemphasis on the reflexive moment in contrast to history.[41] Transcendentality and history are only understood in terms of their respectively distinctive relevance to one another, a necessary relation of reciprocal dependence and conditioning, and in terms of their significance for human experience.

A human being essentially perfects and realizes his existence in history. As such, he is necessarily dependent upon experience and cannot dismiss this in some rationalistic fashion as "unessential," since he has "his eternal essence as something given and handed over to his freedom and reflection, because he experiences, endures, and acts out his history."[42] Our transcendental experience and knowledge is thus always an a posteriori matter from the outset insofar "as every transcendental experience is initially mediated by a categorial encounter with concrete reality in our world, in our (historical) environment [*Umwelt*] and world with others [*Mitwelt*]."[43]

This status of being referred to the concrete experience of history is transcendentally necessary and, as far as the knowing subject is concerned, unavoidable, revealing itself not least in the fact that the transcendental subject conceives himself as a fundamentally finite quantity, despite the fact that his transcendentality is, in principle, unlimited. In other words, the transcendental subject conceives himself as, to be sure, an unlimited open horizon which, however, in the final analysis remains hollow and empty without the categorial experience of the historical object which comes to him from without. The transcendental subject thus always experiences himself as "an open, of itself empty question, as the ecstatic referredness to . . . what he himself precisely is not, since he experiences his transcendentality coming to himself as mediated by experience of the object which on its own terms reveals or conceals itself and of which the subject is not master."[44]

As a consequence, given the finitude of the human spirit, human transcendentality is never objectifiable as far as what it is "in itself," but is always present in a historically categorial mediation.[45] In this connection Rahner speaks of necessary "interpretations" or "categorial objectifications" in which the phenomenon of transcendentality manifests itself, without disappearing in them.[46]

With that, however, the reverse side of this relation is also suggested. Should the human being be able to recognize and realize historical events as "facts" that concern him as a whole and to which he is necessarily and unavoidably referred and related in his existential depths, and should it become unconditionally clear to him thereby that precisely this historically concrete reality must actually concern and affect him in his existence and subjectivity, then this can only happen, Rahner is convinced, in a transcendental reflection. Just as transcendentality first comes to itself in the historical mediation, so also will concrete history in its existentially necessary relevance to human beings first become adequately recognizable in a transcendental inquiry. "The existential significance of historical facts (that is to say, their significance insofar as it affects the entire human being in regard to his salvation) cannot be made understandable at all without transcendental theology."[47]

The Historicity of Revelation and Its Transcendental Grounding Back in the Subject

The irreducible bi-polarity of transcendentality and categoriality in human experience that has been presented demonstrates its relevance on a genuinely theological terrain when—as Rahner intends—it is applied to the question of the epistemological mediation between the historical, divine revelation and the human capacity to receive this revelation, a capacity that is constituted in a transcendentally a priori manner. "The suggested problem of the relation between transcendentally-a priori and categorially-historical-a posteriori theology . . . first acquires its entire profundity and pointedness when it is considered that in theology the ultimate, a priori condition of theological knowledge in the subject, that is to say, grace (which in the last analysis is God acting freely and communicating Himself in history), is the authentic content or, better, the objective basis of what is known a posteriori and historically; when it is considered, accordingly, that the a priori character of the subject and the a posteriori character of the historical object have here in theology a unique relationship that does not surface anywhere else."[48]

If in this relationship, on the one hand, the "transcendental revelation" based on the "supernatural existential" of grace forms the necessarily a priori, foregoing horizon, the *causa formalis*, as it were, for the capacity to hear the good news of revelation, then, on the other hand, the word of God, in its historical concreteness and underivability, dispatching itself in history, forms the material condition and cause, the *causa materialis* of the factual event of revelation. Without a word of historical revelation of the latter sort the human being would still, to be sure, always be referred to the "unspeakable mystery," but would not know whether the mysterious God ultimately opens Himself to or conceals Himself from His creation. The former—according to K. H. Weger's interpretation—"may well be hoped for, but not proven on the philosophical plane of thought, so that really everything depends upon a divine revelation and, in this sense, the human being is a 'hearer of the word.' "[49]

Rahner's early work, *Hearers of the Word*,[50] presents itself, to be sure, merely as a "pretheological grounding of theology"[51] and reckons with, as it were, an "open place" in the human being's a priori constitution. This "open place" is then necessarily filled, but in a way that, due to divine freedom and the word of revelation, is gratuitous and nothing that the human can demand. Nevertheless, already here there is the suggestion of a clear awareness of the problem of the aporia involved in a one-sided determination of the relation between the a priori character and history. To a certain extent, the program of the "transcendental analysis of *Dasein*," announced in the preface to *Hearers of the Word*, already quite clearly proceeds from the fact that the transcendentally a priori character is referred to history. For it "recognizes God as the freely unknown and conceives the human being as an historical entity on the basis of its transcendental subjectivity, referring him in this historicity to his history and commanding him to obey this free, unknown God's word of revelation in his history if it happens to present itself."[52]

As a consequence, on the basis of this fundamental insight into the way that transcendentality and history are reciprocally referred to one another, there emerges in Karl Rahner's understanding of the matter a limitation on the determination of transcendental theology. "It cannot and thereby will not be the theology, but rather a moment of it since theology . . . should always articulate the historically concrete in its underivability."[53] With a view to the historical dimension of the event of Christ, Rahner expresses this elementary referredness with pointed clarity: "The genuine encounter with God happens in history!"[54]

In contrast to the early conception of human transcendentality as *potentia oboedientialis* (that still dominated the discussion in *Hearers of the Word*), the later concept, namely, the concept of the *supernatural existential*, acquired from the realm of the theological relation of nature and grace, signifies at the same time a concretion and a refinement of Rahner's understanding of revelation. Through the transposition of the point of departure for divine revelation to the transcendentally a priori structure of the human essence, the supernatural, categorially historical revelation of God, the Word of God, and the likewise supernaturally constituted transcendentally-a priori dimension of human subjectivity's experience, that is to say, the supernatural existential, are brought together into a synthesis in the event of revelation.

Rahner is convinced that this transcendental theory of knowledge of the process of revelation also offers valuable aspects of interpretation with respect to the points of departure for explanation in further inquiries in the theology of revelation. Our humanly concupiscent cognitive situation, on the one hand, is constantly mediated by the experience of *creatureliness* and, on the other hand, is obscured by the history of human guilt. As a result, the understanding of revelation without the gift of grace would always be either depraved or simply impossible. Insofar as this is the case, Rahner sees in human transcendentality constituted by grace a "supernatural existential." This supernatural existential is the only conceivable point of departure as much in the ideal case of arriving at an essentially pure interpretation of the categorial message of revelation as in making the binding relevance of the word of God plausible to the subject capable of receiving it. What theologians in a first approach call simply "revelation" thus becomes, in Rahner's transcendental theory of revelation, analogously understandable as "the most successful case of the necessary self-interpretation of transcendental revelation."[55]

With this conclusion Rahner has achieved two things. First, by virtue of the grounding of revelation in the transcendental subject as the *supernatural existential*, the legitimation of the point of departure for a transcendentally-anthropological theology is shown in correspondence with the historical category of revelation. For, by means of the transcendental unity of the content of revelation and the transcendental act of receiving that content, the Word of God, on the one hand, and the hearing subject, on the other, are not alien quantities. Second, the a posteriori form of revelation and therein, in particular, the unsurpassable high point of God's communication of Himself in Jesus Christ—the hypostatic union between God and the human being—can be intelligibly presented as the absolute presupposition and only certain, essentially pure and complete interpretation of supernatural transcendentality and as existentially unavoidable.

In unity with the historically mediated encounter with the Gospel, the transcendental constitution of the human being thus forms an ultimately "indissoluble circle,"[56] to the effect that, as K. H. Weger puts it, "in the encounter with the Gospel something is also said to me that I can in no way say to myself and yet is the hoped-for, unrealized fulfillment of my life."[57]

"Lessing's Difficulty" and the Logic of Existential Knowledge

As has already been suggested, the aporia in the relation between transcendentality and categoriality, that is to say, between the a priori, universal structure of knowledge and its contingent historical structure, is expressed in what is commonly and platitudinously characterized as "Lessing's difficulty" with any revealed religion. That difficulty presents itself in the form of the acute question, widespread since the Enlightenment, of how revealed truths that result from historical events can lay claim to binding validity when brought before the tribunal of human reason, the nature of which is "universal" and has been elevated to a theoretical level. Transposed to Christianity as an explicitly revealed religion, the question has the following significance: how can a religion and doctrine, that have arisen historically, lay claim to being necessary to the salvation of all human beings? And, vice versa, in view of the universal, sacred will of God, how can those realities—those constituting the content of Christianity and obtaining therein, in the way explained, as the basic pillars necessary for salvation—be fixed and limited to the historical realm of validation and the completion in faith of a contingent, historically revealed religion? Although this may at first glance appear to be a secondary, marginal problem, Rahner attempts to provide a solution to this *mysterium iniquitatis* in the proper sense against the backdrop of the Ignatian exercises by developing his "logic of existential knowledge."[58]

In his "Spiritual Exercises," Ignatius posed the problem of how a human being, in the context of the personal situation of a decision, could constitute the concrete will of God for this existential, historical situation of that person's very own life. Because of its rigorously causal and, thus, supra-individual, general way of thinking, the traditional and classical Aristotelian logic is as powerless in the face of this problem as it is when confronted with "Lessing's difficulty." For Ignatius, a way out of the dilemma presents itself via the introduction of one's own "existential logic" in which the experience of a "nonobjective consolation," the *consolación sin causa* in the Exercises, allows the will of God in the situation to be known. What is involved, thereby, is an experience that is "nonobjective," but existential and becoming thematic, namely, the experience of a harmony with the "goal" and "direction" [*Woraufhin*] of human transcendence, in which the object of the human being's choice becomes evident to him or her in an existential manner. "Thus, the experience of the reciprocal congruence between the historically finite object of choice, on the one hand, and the pure opening to transcendence, on the other, becomes what makes it possible to know the historical, individual will of God."[59]

Here an existential logic, applicable to the concrete historical objects of personal choice, takes the place of abstract, universal principles, as are applied in the system of thought of the Aristotelian, causal logic. The most important effect of this existential logic lies in its applicability to historical events that are significant in an existential manner and to fatefully experienced situations of decision in the personal life of a human being. Thanks to this new way of thinking, the form of thinking is transformed. What matters are questions and answers appropriate to the subjective point of reference of an existential decision, that is to say, to the human being in the situation of a personal, free choice, in contrast to a way of thinking in terms of causality, necessarily reducing the concrete circumstances of life to some universal.

In an analogous fashion, Rahner attempts to reach a similar moment by applying the transcendental manner of thinking in the context of the theology of revelation. Insofar as the human being, on the basis of his transcendentality, is the "event of God's communication of Himself,"[60] the human being stands in a relation to the ground of his existence, a relation that constitutes him in an existentially decisive sense as a "pre-conscious hearer" of revelation. The historical contents of the faith are thus never wholly novel to him, as though they appear from without as the effect of something utterly alien. Instead, the hearing of revelation in itself signifies an introduction to something with which we are already embryonically acquainted, a coming-to-oneself, a knowing that is already present in a rudimentary way. Revelation is a way of becoming conscious of what has already been known for quite some time and can thereby be pursued in its essence as "mystagogy," an introduction into the mystery to which the human being himself is already essentially referred. The revelation, so understood, only unfolds what is implicitly inherent in things, so that the assumption can appear to the subject as "existentially logical" and "necessary."[61]

Overview: The Foundation of the Anthropological Point of Departure in Transcendental Theology

As far as the methical execution of Rahner's theology with its anthropological point of departure is concerned, it presents itself explicitly as a formally transcendental theology and implicitly as a materially transcendental theology. The aim is to pursue theology as a "transcendental reflection," by constantly turning back to the subject and its a priori conditions of knowing. The transcendental, a priori moment of theology is to be developed here in an integral synthesis with the historical, categorial dimension of theology. By this means, transcendental anthropology and transcendental theology of revelation, along with all the historical, categorial implications of the latter, ideally come together, mediated by the central concept in the theory of transcendental theology: the concept of a *supernatural existential*. The transcendentally theological reflection on the conditions of historical revelation thereby merges with the transcendentally anthropological reflection on the conditions of human experience of the self—since this reflection is finalized by theology. Because the condition of the possibility of revelation and that of human experience of the self is one and the same condition—namely, the "transcendental essence" of a human being in her individuality and entirety—the result of both must be the same. This implies, as a logical consequence, the possibility and the legitimacy of that "transcendentally anthropological turn" postulated and carried out by Rahner. For the same reason, as a transcendentally theological manner of thinking, this turn must realize its anthropological point of departure.

NOTES

1. "Gnade als Mitte menschlicher Existenz," Interview mit Karl Rahner, *Herder Korrespondenz* 28 (1974): 83.

2. K. Rahner, "Transzendentaltheologie," *Herders Theologisches Taschenlexikon*, ed. K. Rahner (Freiburg: Herder, 1973), 7: 324 (see also 325–29). Regarding aspects of the definition, see also K. Rahner, "Transzendentaltheologie," *Sacramentum Mundi* (Freiburg: Herder, 1960), 4: 986–92, especially 986, and "Überlegungen zur Methode der Theologie," *Schriften zur Theologie* 9 (1970): 95–113, especially 96. On the question of the foundation, see J. B. Lotz, *Transzendentale Erfahrung* (Freiburg: Herder, 1978).

3. See the already cited passage from Kant's *Kritik der reinen Vernunft*, B 25.

4. K. Rahner, "Theologie und Anthropologie," *Schriften zur Theologie* 8 (1967): 44.

5. For an understanding of the interpretive and methodological difficulties regarding this connection, a preliminary but adequate understanding of the concepts employed by Rahner is fundamental. In this context, it is particularly necessary from the outset to indicate the expansiveness of the definition of "transcendental philosophy" as well as the transformation, at least partially, of the content of the concept, which a series of

newly added elements brings with it. In a rather undifferentiated adaptation of the concept, Rahner designates as "transcendental philosophy" even that neo-scholastic epistemology which proceeds on the basis of the central Kantian starting point of the so-called "transcendental" regressive inquiry into the conditions of the possibility of knowledge in the subject and attempts, on its own, to synthesize this procedure with Thomas Aquinas' metaphysics of knowledge and its distinctive feature of being centered in the doctrine of the transcendentals. On this point, see K. Rahner, *Geist in Welt*. In addition to Rahner's own position, see above all the extensive presentation in O. Muck, *Die transzendentale methode in der scholastischen Philosophie der Gegenwart* (Innsbruck: F. Rauch, 1964) and R. Schaeffler, *Die Wechselbeziehungen zwischen Philosophie und katholischer Theologie* (Darmstadt: Wissenschaftliche Buchgesellschaft, 1980), 187–228. W. Hoerers takes a polemical and critical stand against this "neoscholastically modified" concept of "transcendental philosophy," especially the Rahnerian version; see W. Hoerers, "Rahner und Kant—Von der Metaphysik zur 'Auslegung der Subjektivität,' " *Theologisches* 185 (1985): 6586–92 and *Kritik der transzendentalphilosophischen Erkenntnistheorie* (Stuttgart: Kohlhammer, 1969). Finally, a further line of the expansion of the content of the concept "transcendental philosophy" is set in motion principally by J. Maréchal's *Le point de départ de la métaphysique* which with its conception of Kant pointed the way for Rahner's transcendental conception. Noteworthy at this juncture is also the reference to J. B. Lotz's *Transzendentale Erfahrung*, a work which, in a way analogous to Rahner's, reaches back to the thought of Maréchal and concerns itself with developing transcendental thinking further in the light of a far-reaching interpretation of the transcendental unity of Kantian apperception.

    6. K. Rahner, "Überlegungen zur Methode der Theologie," *Schriften zur Theologie* 9 (1970): 96.

    7. Ibid.

    8. G.W.F. Hegel, *Phänomenologie des Geistes*, ed. J. Hoffmeister (Hamburg: Meiner, 1952), 63.

    9. K. Rahner, "Überlegungen zur Methode der Theologie," *Schriften zur Theologie* 9 (1970): 96.

    10. K. Rahner, "Transzendentaltheologie," *Sacramentum Mundi* (Freiburg: Herder, 1969), 4: 986.

11. Ibid., 987.
12. K. Rahner, "Über künftige Wege der Theologie," *Schriften zur Theologie* 10(1972): 55.
13. K. Rahner, *Grundkurs*, 36 (25). See also K. Rahner, "Überlegungen zur Methode der Theologie," *Schriften zur Theologie* 9 (1970): 95–102, especially 101: "If in this sense philosophy is necessarily transcendental philosophy (even though the thematizing of its genuine essence is first accomplished later in the history of philosophy), and if, further, theology given its very essence is necessarily also philosophical theology because otherwise it would be belief and confession, but no longer theology (indeed, it would not even be really belief and confession any more), then it is basically self-evident that theology must be transcendental theology."
14. L. B. Puntel, "Zu den Begriffen 'transzendental' und 'kategorial' bei Karl Rahner," *Wagnis Theologie: Erfahrungen mit der Theologie Karl Rahners*, 192.
15. K. Rahner, "Theologie und Anthropologie," *Schriften zur Theologie* 8 (1967): 45.
16. On this systematic separation, carried out by Kant, and on the "deep gulf" between theoretical and practical reason, projected by this means, see above, Chapter 1, Division Two, Section One.
17. I. Kant, *Kritik der reinen Vernunft*, B 25.
18. K. Rahner, "Überlegungen zur Methode der Theologie," *Schriften zur Theologie* 9 (1970): 98.
19. K. Rahner, "Theologie und Anthropologie," *Schriften zur Theologie* 8 (1967): 50.
20. Ibid.
21. K. Rahner, *Grundkurs*, 31 (19–20).
22. K. Rahner, "Überlegungen zur Methode der Theologie," *Schriften zur Theologie* 9 (1970): 99. In another passage Rahner remarks: "The experience of God intended here is of transcendental necessity. Were this . . . denied, then God would be understood as an arbitrary object, the experience of whom by the human being could be just as legitimately indulged or avoided." See K. Rahner, "Kirchliche und außerkirchliche Religiosität," *Schriften zur Theologie* 12 (1975): 589.
23. K. Rahner, *Grundkurs*, 32 (20).
24. For this view, see F. Greiner, *Die Menschlichkeit der Offenbar-*

ung: *Die transzendentale Grundlegung der Theologie bei Karl Rahner* (Munich: Kaiser, 1978), 116–29; also W. Hoerers, "Rahner und Kant—Von der Metaphysik zur 'Auslegung der Subjektivität,' " and *Kritik der transzendentalphilosophischen Erkenntnistheorie.*

25. K. Rahner, "Wort Gottes," *Lexikon für Theologie und Kirche,* 10, 2nd ed. (Freiburg: Herder, 1965), 1236.

26. K. Rahner, "Theologie und Anthropologie," *Schriften zur Theologie* 8 (1967): 51.

27. K. Rahner, *Grundkurs,* 32 (20–21).

28. Ibid., 45 (34).

29. On this synthesis, compare the analogous interest guiding knowledge in the case of J. B. Lotz, *Transzendentale Erfahrung.*

30. K. Rahner, *Grundkurs,* 63 (54).

31. K. Rahner, "Überlegungen zur Methode der Theologie," *Schriften zur Theologie* 9 (1970): 99.

32. Ibid.

33. K. Rahner, *Grundkurs,* 64 (55).

34. Ibid.

35. Ibid., 79 (71).

36. K. Rahner, "Anthropologie. Theologische Anthropologie," 177.

37. Ibid., 178.

38. K. Rahner, "Theologie und Anthropologie," *Schriften zur Theologie* 8 (1967): 53. An understanding closely analogous to Rahner's understanding of his central problematic of a reciprocal, "dynamic" relation of subjectivity and objectivity, of the "in itself" and "for itself" in the absolute "in and for itself" of God, is presented in Hegel's *Phenomenology of Spirit.*

39. K. Rahner, "Überlegungen zur Methode der Theologie," *Schriften zur Theologie* 9 (1970): 99.

40. K. Rahner, "Gnade als Mitte menschlicher Existenz," *Herder Korrespondenz* 28 (1974): 83.

41. K. Rahner, *Grundkurs,* 51 (40).

42. Ibid.

43. Ibid., 61 (52).

44. K. Rahner, "Überlegungen zur Methode der Theologie," *Schriften zur Theologie* 10 (1970): 99.

45. This corresponds to the basic anthropological formula of Rahner's philosophical "early period," which defines the

human being as the "spirit in the world"; see K. Rahner, *Geist in Welt*. In spite of the philosophically untenable thesis of the interpretation of Thomas Aquinas presented therein, particular note should be taken of the aspect of the finitude of human knowledge as it is indicated in this work on the basis of the humanly restricted spirituality "in the world."

46. See K. Rahner, *Grundkurs*, 47 (37) and elsewhere. Kant employed the pair of concepts "categorial" and "transcendental" as gnoseological quantities for the characterization of *a priori* and *a posteriori* elements of knowledge. For Rahner, by contrast (in the wake of Heidegger's existential ontology), they acquire hermeneutical significance as anthropological quantities characterizing the existential perfection of the human being. In this regard see especially L. B. Puntel, "Zu den Begriffen 'transzendental' und 'kategorial' bei Karl Rahner," in *Wagnis Theologie*, 189–98. If Rahner defines the "transcendental" loosely as the sum of what, mediated by subjectivity, is necessarily universal in diametrical contrast to the "categorial" as the sum of what has unfolded in a finitely specific and contingently historical manner, then "the profoundest aporiai of Rahner's thinking [present themselves] in the conceptual instruments 'categorial'—'transcendental'," as K. Lehman puts it in his "Rahner-Portrait"; see K. Lehmann, "Karl Rahner," *Bilanz der Theologie im 20. Jahrhundert*, 4:169n.18.

47. K. Rahner, "Überlegungen zur Methode der Theologie," *Schriften zur Theologie* 9 (1970): 112.

48. K. Rahner, "Theologie und Anthropologie," *Schriften zur Theologie* 8 (1967): 45.

49. K. H. Weger, *Karl Rahner. Eine Einführung in sein theologisches Denken*, 66.

50. K. Rahner, *Hörer des Wortes*. In order to allow Rahner's genuine insight to express itself in each instance, the original 1941 version, here cited, is to be consulted over against the revision of this work by J. B. Metz, published as the second edition (Munich: Kösel, 1963).

51. K. Rahner, *Hörers des Wortes*, 29.

52. Ibid., 27f.

53. K. Rahner, "Überlegungen zur Methode der Theologie," *Schriften zur Theologie* 9 (1970): 112.

54. K. Rahner, *Ich glaube an Jesus Christus* (Einsiedeln: Benziger, 1968), 33.

55. K. Rahner, *Grundkurs*, 159 (155).

56. In this connection it is not possible to address the question of the extent to which this "indissoluble circle" is, nevertheless, dissolved by Rahner in the discussion of the problematic of the "anonymous Christian." On this question of a possibility of salvation even for non-Christians, a question which at least since Vatican II has established itself in theology as a general problem for Christianity, reference may be made simply to the plethora of literature on this *Quaestio disputata*. The *status quaestionis* consists, indeed, in the question of how a salvation for non-Christians is thinkable in view of the explained "necessity" of the revelation of Christ for "salvation" [*Heilsnotwendigkeit*] or, putting it otherwise, how the non-Christian's hope for salvation, resting on "only" natural revelation, could become a possibility for the salvation that is only thinkable in Christ.

57. K. H. Weger, *Karl Rahner. Eine Einführung in sein theologisches Denken*, 108.

58. See K. Rahner, "Die Logik der existentiellen Erkenntnis bei Ignatius von Loyola," in *Das Dynamische in der Kirche* (= *Quaestiones disputatae* 5) (Freiburg: Herder, 1958), 74–148. Rahner's interpretation of Ignatius is otherwise regarded suspiciously and not even recognized by some critics. Nevertheless, this very contribution to the interpretation of the *consolación sin causa precedente* "is also shared by those who otherwise do not agree with his interpretation of Ignatius' text." On this matter see J. C. Scannone, "Die Logik des Existentiellen und Geschichtlichen nach Karl Rahner," in *Wagnis Theologie. Erfahrungen mit der Theologie Karl Rahners*, 83.

59. J. C. Scannone, "Die Logik des Existentiellen und Geschichtlichen nach Karl Rahner," in *Wagnis Theologie: Erfahrungen mit der Theologie Karl Rahners*, 88.

60. K. Rahner, *Grundkurs*, 122.

61. In this "mystagogical" understanding of revelation, echoes of the "anamnesis" model of the Platonic tradition are patent. In this regard, K. Lehman remarks: "It is clear that underlying this problem are the ancient Platonic differentiation of an ideal realm from reality as well as the difficult relation between the 'historical' and 'theological' method. The acute question, already rampant for more than 200 years, is at bottom not answered even in the present day; indeed, it is not even

correctly formulated. In view of this history of the problem, it is not astonishing that even Rahner's thinking at this juncture comes to a final aporia." See K. Lehmann, "Karl Rahner, Ein Portrait," in K. Lehmann/A. Raffelt (eds.), *Rechenschaft des Glaubens. Karl Rahner-Lesebuch*, 50*–51*.

EXCURSUS: ON THE RELATION OF PHILOSOPHY AND THEOLOGY AGAINST THE BACKDROP OF "TRANSCENDENTAL REVELATION"

FROM THE PRECEDING PRESENTATION it should be evident how much Karl Rahner, in elaborating a transcendental-theological basis for theology, builds on philosophical foundations. The following excursus, though naturally limited to a few suggestions, attempts to point out how Rahner became increasingly clearer about philosophy and theology and attained an ever more nuanced determination of the relationship between them. While the somewhat naïve determination of the *potentia oboedientialis* in *Hearers of the Word* marks the point of departure for his thinking,[1] his subsequent reflection on the relation of nature and grace led to a clearly differentiated combination and connection of philosophical and theological self-understanding in a "supernatural existential."

I. THE EARLY THESIS IN *HEARERS OF THE WORD*

The Human Being as potentia oboedientialis of Divine Revelation

The basic idea underlying *Hearers of the Word* is to conceive human beings as *potentia oboedientialis* for a possible self-communication on God's part in history. With this basic idea in hand, Rahner presupposes a fundamental relation between the natural, philosophical capacity of human beings to hear and the divine revelation. "God can only reveal what human beings can hear."[2]

Taking his start from the actuality and facticity of revelation in history, Rahner reflects on the philosophical and anthropological conditions of the possibility of a capacity in the receptive subject to accept and even embrace things. By this means he is able to explain why human beings, by virtue of the nature proper to them, are disposed to something like revelation at all.[3] To put the matter differently, a constitutive openness to God must be posited at the core of human nature, given with the very essence of being human. This openness must transport human beings into a position of being able to identify God's revelation as such, transpiring in history, and thus become "hearers of the word." The "foundation of a philosophy of religion" that is intended in *Hearers of the Word* is to be understood as a project that can be made "only with the natural light of reason" (at least as Rahner conceived matters at the time), since philosophical anthropology, on the one hand, and fundamental theological anthropology, on the other, seamlessly coincide in this project, as do nature and grace as well as theology and philosophy (as the condition of the possibility of theology).[4] According to *Hearers of the Word*, "philosophy's last word," since it makes its way with "purely philosophical means," is the thematization of "the imperative to obey God's word."[5]

In this conception, viewed as a whole, the word of God enters into a conditional relation to the human openness to this word, an openness that is to be attributed to the human spirit itself as a "natural" part of its makeup. By this route, however, grace falls under the law of nature. The questionableness of such a point of departure and the difficulty arising from it for the relation of a "purely natural" philosophy and a theology "determined by revelation" are described by K. P. Fischer in the following manner: "According to *Hearers of the Word*, the created spirit can only 'await' ever new positings or deeds by God as possible in the constitution of the creature itself. A completely new grounding of this spiritual existence itself, a self-communication and self-commitment on the part of the grounding mystery, does not lie within the horizon of the *potentia oboedientialis* of *Hearers of the Word*."[6]

II. THE REVISED CONCEPTION IN THE *FOUNDATIONS OF CHRISTIAN FAITH*

The Synthesis of Philosophical Knowledge and Transcendental Revelation in the Supernatural Existential

Struck by the aporia presented in the last section, Rahner arrived at a revised determination of the relation between philosophy and theology, nature and grace, a determination that he set down for the first time with some degree of clarity in his article "Philosophy and Theology."[7] As "the basic formula of human self-understanding," philosophy forms a basic unity unto itself in advance of revelation. For this reason, the acceptance of revelation must play itself off as a confrontation of the divine word and human thinking, of theology and philosophy. This insight prods Rahner to take up the demand of making not only the fact of revelation but all its contents constantly answerable to the forum of thinking. On the one hand, if "the fact of the revelation of the word were psychologically so absolutely apparent and compelling that no doubt were possible at all, then one could prop up its content in a positivistic manner as a mystery that is not to be discussed."[8] On the other hand, there is an obligation "to trust human beings to be able, on the basis of the content of the dogma itself, to believe it with intellectual honesty."[9]

Rahner recognizes that the only viable path for theology is to start out anthropologically, that only in this way is theology in a position of indicating the connection between the self-experience of human beings that is to be raised to new heights philosophically and the content of theological propositions. In order, however, that this dependency, in view of a widespread understanding of philosophy, not be detrimental to "the dignity and autonomy of revelation and theology," Rahner proposes as a solution "that the revelation as the supreme entelechy and norm . . . presupposes this alien 'philosophical' knowledge precisely as its other as the condition for its own possibility."[10]

To iterate: there are two, initially contrary claims to a philosophical self-understanding in advance of revelation. On the one hand, it must be "naturally" constituted, that is, it must spring from a criterion independent of revelation and thus outside theology. On the other hand, it must still be of "supernatural" origin in order not to subordinate grace to the law of nature. Rahner synthesizes these two contrary claims in the "supernatural existential," on the basis of which the human and "naturally philosophical transcendentality" is always already centered in the event of grace. By this means, "pure" philosophy remains thinkable exclusively in the sense that, while not drawing or borrowing any material content from the historically given revelation, it is not possible for it to spring from the natural essence of human beings, "pure" of grace's unthematic, transcendental illumination of existence. For an authentic philosophizing, it also follows from the concept of the "supernatural existential" that "every philosophy is already and unavoidably pursuing theology without thematizing it."[11]

Lying in the background of this insight is Rahner's already mentioned determination of the relation between natural and supernatural realms. Nature is in itself always a "deficient mode" of the supernatural and first comes into the fullness of its essential character in the supernatural. Accordingly, from the negation of the transpiring of a "pure" nature, the negation of the possibility of a "pure" philosophy (in a corresponding sense) necessarily follows. At the same time, this conception of subjectivity hearing the revelation occasions a new understanding of the concept of revelation itself. Corresponding to the supernatural yet historically conceptual and discursive revelation is an equally supernatural yet transcendentally universal revelation in which every human being has a share. "This universal revelation does not occur immediately in the human word of objectivity and conceptuality that thematizes its content, but through an alteration of the unthematic horizon and the spiritually personal, basic disposedness, an alteration which is necessarily given by the acceptance or rejection of the grace supernaturally given."[12]

These ruminations have consequences for the unity of nature and grace as well as that of philosophy and theology. To every external, historical revelation there is a corresponding internal component of supernatural, transcendental experience in human beings.[13] This correspondence is such that revelation in itself (and thereby theological knowledge generally) is always a holistic act, "an experience of correspondence between the external and internal word of God, an experience made possible by grace."[14] This fundamental relation proper to revelational theology has immediate relevance for the necessity and significance of the "transcendentally-anthropological starting point" of theology. Rahner captures this relevance with the following programmatic formulation: "The coinciding of such connections between the content of dogmatic sentences and the human self-experience is, at bottom, nothing other than the required turn to a transcendental-anthropological method in theology."[15]

NOTES

1. K. Rahner, *Hörer des Wortes. Zur Grundlegung einer Religionsphilosophie* (Munich: Kösel, 1941).
2. Ibid., 142. It should be obvious, merely from the formulation cited here, how much the basic point of departure of *Hearers of the Word* would necessarily bring upon itself theological criticism, in particular, the reproach of diminishing, even reducing the power of theology's theme to a dimension of anthropology.
3. According to E. Simons, Rahner supposes that revelation is determined by the human horizon of hearing. See his *Philosophie der Offenbarung in Auseinandersetzung mit "Hörer des Worts" von Karl Rahner*. In contrast to Simons' views, it is necessary to insist that Rahner constantly presupposes the *factum* of revelation and only infers the conditions of hearing in the subject from that presupposition and not vice versa! He is not thereby pursuing a "philosophy of revelation," but rather, in the strict sense of the term, a "philosophy of the ability to hear the revelation."
4. K. Rahner, *Hörer des Wortes*, 211.
5. Ibid.
6. K. P. Fischer, *Der Mensch als Geheimnis: Die Anthropologie Karl Rahners*, 220.
7. K. Rahner, "Philosophie und Theologie," *Schriften zur Theologie* 6 (1965): 91–103. This essay goes back to a lecture held in 1961.
8. K. Rahner, "Theologie und Anthropologie," *Schriften zur Theologie* 8 (1967): 59.
9. K. Rahner, *Grundkurs*, 23 (12).
10. K. Rahner, "Philosophie und Theologie," *Schriften zur Theologie* 6 (1965): 94.
11. Ibid., 100.
12. K. Rahner, "Philosophie und Theologie," *Schriften zur Theologie* 6 (1965): 99.
13. In this regard, see the distinction drawn between "categorial" and "transcendental" revelation; K. Rahner, *Grundkurs*, 175–77 (172–74).
14. K. H. Weger, *Karl Rahner: Eine Einführung in sein theologisches Denkens*, 92.
15. K. Rahner, "Theologie und Anthropologie," *Schriften zur Theologie* 8 (1967): 61.

POSTSCRIPT: IS TRANSCENDENTAL ANTHROPOLOGY THE ADEQUATE FORM FOR CONTEMPORARY THEOLOGY?

RAHNER'S ULTIMATE CONCERN is the fundamental connection between theology and anthropology, nature and grace, and believing and thinking. This connection has been accurately captured by Franz Rosenzweig in his essay, "The New Thinking." "Theological questions," he writes, "must be translated into human ones, and human questions must be pursued until they enter the theological arena."

Not a symmetric identity, but instead a mutual conditioning and interpretive reciprocity characterize the relation between theology and anthropology. Anthropology rests upon the necessity of a grounding that has been "pursued until it enters the theological arena." And theology—today more than ever—is in need of an anthropological hermeneutics.

Karl Rahner gives this elementary requirement its due by carrying out the "transcendentally anthropological turn" in theology (sketched in this study) and, in tune with the basic interest of modern philosophy, by bringing human subjectivity with its claim to freedom and its significance for epistemology into the structure of contemporary theological research. At the same time, however, he makes it clear that subjectivity is something that is constantly transmitted, something with an origin, and thus something referred to and dependent upon the phenomenon of transcendence. In this way Rahner overcomes the temptation to introduce the anthropological starting point in a narrowly immanentistic way. Only when theology, "in the highest reflexive transcendental rationality, shows that the referredness to and dependence upon the absolute mystery is the condition of the possibility of all transparent rationality,"[1] is the groundwork laid for an epistemology capable of sustaining theology. Only in this manner is, on the one hand, a way opened up to regain philosophically an authentic experience of transcendence and, on the other hand, a new synthesis of philosophy and theology made possible—a synthesis suited to epoch-making thinking which, in the final analysis, first permits a belief with "intellectual honesty."[2]

There are two sorts of advantages to be gained from Rahner's transcendental and anthropological foundation of theology, with its emphatically philosophical orientation. In the first place, it rejects all fundamentalistic currents that deny any sort of connection between believing and thinking, philosophy and theology. In the second place, it provides handy and accessible criteria in contrast to one-sided rationalistic and positivistic concepts of modern philosophy (which in itself is anything but a unified movement), concepts in which the realm of knowledge is supposed to be reduced to an objectively verifiable "state of affairs" or an "instance of a rule," and theological knowledge is dismissed from the outset.

Yet, for all its merits, Rahner's anthropological turn in theology is not unproblematic. Despite the wide range of things that can be accomplished with this approach, questions remain on several fronts.

As already suggested, there exists from the outset the fundamental aporia of an adequate mediation between a priori and a posteriori levels, between rationality and history. The difficulties in this regard lead all too easily to a collapse of history into some sort of transcendental deduction. (Or should we say: a reduction of history to a "history of transcendentality"?)

At the same time, the transcendentally anthropological approach of this thinking appears to require a basic feature or move that is individualistic and that would have to be overcome by expanding it in a dialogical direction. If, as Martin Buber writes, "truth is not in the I, but rather between the I and Thou," then transcendental individuality as the sole point of departure for the reality of the faith would have to be considered more rigorously in the sense of the "dialogical principle" with a view to the communicative and interpersonal constitution of human transcendentality. In particular, the spiritual subject's vocation to be an "anonymous Christian" does not signify an inadmissible "universalization" of what is Christian. Is it not rather the case—in the sense of Joseph Ratzinger's and Hans Urs von Balthasar's criticisms of the basic starting point of Rahner's theology—that ecstasy, that state of being torn away, the existential, decisive turn of faith, is a basic constitutive element of what is Christian?

In full awareness of the utter brevity and fragmentary manner with which these few critical questions have been raised here,[3] I have attempted to conclude my critical study of Karl Rahner's imposing theological project by indicating where there is room for further reflection. The fact that critical questions are to be found at the end of this investigation in no way detracts from the significance and the magnitude of this theology. Instead, ending with questions corresponds—in Rahner's own words—to precisely what bestows meaning on this theology in the most original and appropriate of senses. For "only where one turns to the question of questioning, to thinking about thinking itself, to the topos of knowledge and not simply the objects of knowledge, to transcendence and not simply to what is grasped spatio-temporally within this transcendence, is one precisely on the verge of becoming a religious human being, a *homo religiosus.*"⁴

NOTES

1. K. Rahner, "Überlegungen zur Methode der Theologie," *Schriften zur Theologie* 9 (1970): 114.
2. K. Rahner, *Grundkurs*, 18 (6). Michael Lechner's highly illuminating study, *Die Theologie des Maßes: Studien zur kulturgeschichtlichen Bedeutung der Askese bei Romano Guardini* (St. Ottilien: EOS, 1991), goes to the heart, philosophically and existentially, of the question of the original "place of the human being in the context of being," the question of the anthropological measure in the whole of reality.
3. With the few directions of inquiry that have been suggested here, no attempt is being made to take away the demand for criticism of Rahner's work. That would simply not be possible. For this reason, by way of conclusion, reference may be made to the following critical review: J. Ratzinger, "Vom Verstehen des Glaubens. Anmerkungen zu Rahners *Grundkurs des Glaubens,*" *Theologische Revue* 74 (1978): 177–86. This review is one of the best critical studies of Rahner's work, a kind of "settling of accounts" with the latter in its final, synthesized form in the *Foundations of Christian Faith.* At a high level and at the same time with exacting concision, Ratzinger's review sums up the most important objections to, and points of criticism of, Rahner's theology.
4. K. Rahner, *Grundkurs*, 33–34 (22–23).

BIBLIOGRAPHY

Primary Sources

Dych, William. *Karl Rahner.* Outstanding Christian Thinkers. Collegeville, Minn.: Liturgical Press, 1992.

Raffelt, Karl, and Karl Rahner. "Anthropologie und Theologie." In *Christlicher Glaube in Moderner Gesellschaft.* Vol. 24. Eds. F. Böckle, F. Kaufmann, K. Rahner, and B. Welte. Freiburg: Herder, 1981. Pages 5–56.

Rahner, Karl. "Anthropologie. Theologische Anthropologie." In *Sacramentum Mundi.* Vol. 1. Freiburg: Herder, 1967. Pages 176–86.

———. "Anthropozentrik." In *Lexikon für Theologie und Kirche.* 2nd ed., Vol. 1. Freiburg: Herder, 1957. Pages 632–34.

———. "Auf der Suche nach Zugängen zum Verständnis des gottmenschlichen Geheimnisses Jesu." *Schriften zur Theologie.* Vol. 10. Einsiedeln: Benziger, 1972. Pages 209–14.

———. "Bekenntnis zu Thomas von Aquin." *Schriften zur Theologie.* Vol. 10. Einsiedeln: Benziger, 1972. Pages 11–20.

———. "Christlicher Humanismus." *Schriften zur Theologie.* Vol. 7. Einsiedeln: Benziger, 1967. Pages 239–59.

———. "Christologie im Rahmen des modernen Selbst- und Weltverständnisses." *Schriften zur Theologie.* Vol. 9. Einsiedeln: Benziger, 1970. Pages 227–41.

———. "Christologie heute?" *Schriften zur Theologie.* Vol. 12. Einsiedeln: Benziger, 1975. Pages 353–69.

———. "Das Christentum und der 'neue Mensch.'"

Schriften zur Theologie. Vol. 5., 3rd ed. Einsiedeln: Benziger, 1968. Pages 159–79.

———. "Der Mensch von heute und die Religion." *Schriften zur Theologie.* Vol. 6, 2nd. ed. Einsiedeln: Benziger, 1968. Pages 13–33.

———. "Die ewige Bedeutung der Menschheit Jesu für unser Gottesverhältnis." *Schriften zur Theologie.* Vol. 3, 7th. ed. Einsiedeln: Benziger, 1967. Pages 47–60.

———. "Die Herausforderung der Theologie durch das II. Vatikanische Konzil." *Schriften zur Theologie.* Vol. 8. Einsiedeln: Benziger, 1967. Pages 13–42.

———. "Die Logik der existenziellen Erkenntnis bei Ignatius von Loyola." In *Das Dynamische in der Kirche (= Quaestiones disputatae 5).* Freiburg: Herder, 1958. Pages 74–148.

———. "Die menschliche Sinnfrage vor dem absoluten Geheimnis." *Schriften zur Theologie.* Vol. 13. Einsiedeln: Benziger, 1978. Pages 111–28.

———. "Die theologische Dimension der Frage nach dem Menschen." *Schriften zur Theologie.* Vol. 12. Einsiedeln: Benziger, 1975. Pages 387–406.

———. "Die Zukunft der Theologie." *Schriften zur Theologie.* Vol. 9. Einsiedeln: Benziger, 1970. Pages 148–57.

———. "Einfache Klarstellung zum eigenen Werk." *Schriften zur Theologie.* Vol. 12. Einsiedeln: Benziger, 1975. Pages 599–608.

———. *Encounter with Silence.* Trans. James M. Demske. Westminster, Md.: Newman, 1960.

———. "Experiment Mensch." *Schriften zur Theologie.* Vol. 8. Einsiedeln: Benziger, 1967. Pages 260–85.

———. *Geist in Welt: Zur Metaphysik der endlichen Erkenntnis bei Thomas von Aquin.* 1st ed. Innsbruck and Leipzig: Kösel, 1939; 2nd ed. Munich: Kösel, 1957; 3rd ed. Munich: Kösel: 1964. English translation: *Spirit in the World.* Trans. William V. Dych, S. J. London: Sheed & Ward; New York: Herder & Herder, 1968. (Translation of the 1957 edition.)

———. "Glaubensbegründung heute." *Schriften zur Theologie.* Vol. 12. Einsiedeln: Benziger, 1975. Pages 17–40.

———. "Gotteserfahrung heute." *Schriften zur Theologie.* Vol. 9. Einsiedeln: Benziger, 1970. Pages 161–76.

———. *Grundkurs des Glaubens: Einführung in den Begriff des Christentums.* 11th ed. Freiburg: Herder, 1979. English translation: *Foundations of the Christian Faith: An Introduction to the Idea of Christianity.* Trans. William V. Dych, S. J. New York: Crossroad, 1993.

———. "Grundkurs des Glaubens." *Schriften zur Theologie.* Vol. 14. Einsiedeln: Benziger, 1980. Pages 48–62.

———. "Grundsätzliche Überlegungen zur Anthropologie und Protologie im Rahmen der Theologie." *Mysterium Salutis.* Vol. 2. Einsiedeln: Benziger, 1967. Pages 405–20.

———. *Hörer des Wortes: Zur Grundlegung einer Religionsphilosophie.* 1st ed. Munich: Kösel, 1941. Rev. J. B. Metz. 2nd ed. Munich: Kösel, 1963. English translation: *Hearers of the Word.* Trans. Michael Richards. New York: Herder & Herder, 1969. (Translation of the 1941 edition.)

———. *Ich glaube an Jesus Christus.* Einsiedeln: Benziger, 1968.

———. "Kirchliche und außerkirchliche Religiosität." *Schriften zur Theologie.* Vol. 12. Einsiedeln: Benziger, 1975. Pages 582–98.

———. "Mensch: Zum theologischen Begriff des Menschen." *Sacramentum Mundi.* Vol. 3. Freiburg: Herder, 1969. Pages 396–417.

———. "Mystische Erfahrung und mystische Theologie." *Schriften zur Theologie.* Vol. 12. Einsiedeln: Benziger, 1975. Pages 428–38.

———. "Natur und Gnade." *Schriften zur Theologie.* Vol. 4, 5th ed. Einsiedeln: Benziger, 1967. Pages 209–36.

———. "Philosophie und Theologie." *Schriften zur Theologie.* Vol. 6, 2nd ed. Einsiedeln: Benziger, 1968. Pages 91–103.

———. *Schriften zur Theologie.* Vols. 1–16. Einsiedeln: Benziger, 1954–1980. English translation: *Theological Investigations*. Vols. 1–22. Baltimore: Helicon; New York: Herder & Herder; New York: Seabury/Crossroad; London: Darton, Longman & Todd, 1961–93.

———. "Selbsterfahrung und Gotteserfahrung." *Schriften zur Theologie.* Vol. 10. Einsiedeln: Benziger, 1972. Pages 133–44.

———. "Theologie und Anthropologie." *Schriften zur Theologie.* Vol. 8. Einsiedeln: Benziger, 1967. Pages 43–65.

———. "Transzendentaltheologie." *Herders Theologisches Taschenlexikon.* Ed. Karl Rahner. Vol. 7. Freiburg: Herder, 1973. Pages 324–29.

———. "Transzendentaltheologie." *Sacramentum Mundi.* Vol. 4. Freiburg: Herder, 1969. Pages 986–92.

———. "Über das Verhältnis von Natur und Gnade." *Schriften zur Theologie.* Vol. 1., 2nd ed. Einsiedeln: Benziger, 1967. Pages 323–46.

———. "Über den Begriff des Geheimnisses in der katholischen Theologie." *Schriften zur Theologie.* Vol. 4. Einsiedeln: Benziger, 1967. Pages 51–99.

———. "Über die Einheit von Nächsten- und Gottesliebe." *Schriften zur Theologie.* Vol. 6., 2nd ed. Einsiedeln: Benziger, 1968. Pages 277–98.

———. "Über die Erfahrung der Gnade." *Schriften zur Theologie.* Vol. 3. Einsiedeln: Benziger, 1967. Pages 105–9.

———. "Über die Verborgenheit Gottes." *Schriften zur Theologie.* Vol. 12. Einsiedeln: Benziger, 1975. Pages 285–305.

———. "Über künftige Wege der Theologie." *Schriften zur Theologie.* Vol. 10. Einsiedeln: Benziger, 1972. Pages 41–69.

———. "Überlegungen zur Methode der Theologie." *Schriften zur Theologie.* Vol. 9. Einsiedeln: Benziger, 1970. Pages 79–126.

———. "Wort Gottes." In *Lexikon für Theologie und Kirche.* Vol. 10, 2nd ed. Freiburg: Herder, 1965. Pages 1235–38.

———. "Würde und Freiheit des Menschen." *Schriften zur Theologie.* Vol. 2, 2nd ed. Einsiedeln: Benziger, 1968. Pages 247–77.

———. "Zum Verhältnis zwischen Theologie und heutigen Wissenschaften." *Schriften zur Theologie.* Vol. 10. Einsiedeln: Benziger, 1972. Pages 104–12.

———. "Zum heutigen Verhältnis von Philosophie und Theologie." *Schriften zur Theologie.* Vol. 10. Einsiedeln: Benziger, 1972. Pages 70–88.

———. "Zur Theologie der Menschwerdung." *Schriften zur Theologie.* Vol. 4, 5th ed. Einsiedeln: Benziger, 1967. Pages 137–55.

Rahner, Karl, and H. Rahner. *Worte ins Schweigen–Gebete der Einkehr.* 5th ed. Freiburg: Herder, 1980.

Rahner, Karl, and J. Ratzinger. *Offenbarung und Überlieferung.* Freiburg: Herder, 1965.

Rahner, Karl, and W. Thysing. *Christologie–systematisch und exegetisch: Grundlinien einer systematischen Christologie.* Freiburg: Herder, 1972.

[Karl Rahner]. "Gnade als Mitte menschlicher Existenz. Interview mit Karl Rahner." *Herder Korrespondenz* 28 (1974): 77–92.

[Karl Rahner]. "Lebenslauf." *Der Entschluß: Zeitschrift für Praxis und Theologie* 31 (1977): 30–34.

[Karl Rahner]. "Erfahrungen eines Theologen: Karl Rahner über die Möglichkeiten und Grenzen der Theologie." *Herder Korrespondenz* 38 (1984): 224–30.

[Karl Rahner]. "A Changing Ecclesiology in a Changing Church: A Symposium on Development in the Ecclesiology of Karl Rahner." *Theological Studies* 38 (1977): 736–62.

SECONDARY SOURCES

Amelung, E. "Autonomie." *Theologische Realenzyklopädie.* Vol. 5. Eds. Gerhard Krause and Gerhard Müller. Berlin: de Gruyter, 1980. Pages 4ff.

Aquinas, Thomas. *Quaestiones disputate de veritate, Quaestio 1.* Trans. and ed. Albert Zimmermann. Hamburg: Meiner, 1986.

———. *Truth.* Vol. 1. Trans. R. W. Mulligan. Chicago: Regnery, 1952.

Balthasar, Hans Urs von. *Cordula oder der Ernstfall.* 3rd ed. Einsiedeln: Johannes, 1967.

———. *Glaubhaft ist nur die Liebe.* 4th ed. Einsiedeln: Johannes, 1975.

Bantle, F. X. "Person und Personbegriff in der Trinitätslehre Karl Rahners." *Münchener Theologische Zeitschrift* 30 (1979): 11–24.

Bauerdick, R. "Transzendentale Subjektivität oder Transzendentalität des Subjekts: Die mystische Theologie Karl Rahners am Ende der Moderne." *Freiburger Zeitschrift für Philosophie und Theologie* 33 (1986): 291–310.

Blumenberg, H. "Autonomie." *Religion in Geschichte und Gegenwart: Handwörterbuch für Theologie und Religionswissenschaft.* Ed. Kurt Galling. Vol. 1 (Tübingen: Mohr, 1956): 788ff.

Bokwa, I. *Christologie als Anfang und Ende der Anthropologie: Über das gegenseitige Verhältnis zwischen Christologie und Anthropologie bei Karl Rahner.* Frankfurt and New York: Peter Lang, 1990.

Brechtken, J. "Zur temporalen Interpretation der Gottesfrage bei Metz und Rahner." *Theologie und Glaube* 64 (1974): 146–61.

Broch, T. *Das Problem der Freiheit im Werk von Pierre Teilhard de Chardin.* Mainz: Matthias-Grunewald, 1977.

Corduan, W. "Hegel in Rahner: A Study in Philosophical Hermeneutics." *Harvard Theological Review* 71 (1978): 285–98.

Couto, F. J. "Katholische Theologie: Zu Rahners *Grundkurs des Glaubens.*" *Theologe und Glaube* 67 (1977): 422–31.

Daecke, S. M. "Das Ja und das Nein des Konzils zu Teilhard." In *Die Autorität der Freiheit: Gegenwart des Konzils und Zukunft der Kirche im ökumenischen Disput*. Vol. 3. Ed. J. Ch. Hampe. Munich: Kösel, 1967. Pages 98–112.

Eicher, P. *Die anthropologische Wende: Karl Rahners philosophischer Weg vom Wesen des Menschen zur personalen Existenz*. Freiburg/Schweiz: Universitätsverlag, 1970.

———. "Wovon spricht die transzendentale Theologie? Zur gegenwärtigen Auseinandersetzung um das Denken von Karl Rahner." *Theologische Quartalschrift* 156 (1976): 284–350.

Fabro, C. *La svolta antropologica di Karl Rahner*. Milan: Rusconi, 1974.

Fahlenbusch, E. "Gespräche im realen Humanismus: Karl Rahner (1904–1984)." *Materialdienst des konfessionskundlichen Instituts Bensheim* 35 (1984): 43–45.

———. "Zum Begriff des Christentums." *Materialdienst des konfessionskundlichen Instituts Bensheim* 28 (1977): 36–40.

Fahlenbusch, E. "Karl Rahner: Theologie in der Nachfolge des Thomas von Aquin." *Materialdienst des konfessionskundlichen Instituts Bensheim* 25 (1975): 22–25.

Fischer, K. P. *Der Mensch als Geheimnis: Die Anthropologie des Karl Rahners—Mit einem Brief von Karl Rahner*. Freiburg: Herder, 1974.

———. "Wo der Mensch an das Geheimnis grenzt: Die mystagogische Struktur der Theologie Karl Rahners." *Zeitschrift für Katholische Theologie* 98 (1976): 159–70.

———. "*Grundkurs des Glaubens* (Karl Rahner)." *Theologie und Philosophie* 52 (1977): 67–71.

———. *Gotteserfahrung: Mystagogie in der Theologie Karl Rahners und in der Theologie der Befreiung*. Mainz: Matthias-Grunewald, 1987.

Fries, H. "Theologische Methode bei John Henry Newman und Karl Rahner." *Catholica* 33 (1979): 109–33.

Gadamer, H.G., and Paul Vogler, eds. *Neue Anthropologie*. Vols. 1–7. Stuttgart: Thieme, 1972–74.

Gerken, A. *Offenbarung und Transzendenzerfahrung*. Düsseldorf: Patmos, 1969.

Greiner, F. "Die Menschlichkeit der Offenbarung: Die transzendentale Grundlegung der Theologie bei Karl Rahner im Lichte seiner Christologie." *Zeitschrift für Katholische Theologie* 100 (1978): 596–619.

———. *Die Menschlichkeit der Offenbarung: Die transzendentale Grundlegung der Theologie bei Karl Rahner.* Munich: Kaiser, 1978.

Gruber, L. *Transzendentalphilosophie und Theologie bei Fichte und Rahner.* Frankfurt: Lang, 1978.

Halder, A. "Anthropologie. I. Philosophische Anthropologie." *Staatslexikon.* Vol. 1, 7th ed. Freiburg: Herder, 1985. Pages 169ff.

———. "Person. I. Begriffsgeschichte." *Lexikon für Theologie und Kirche.* Vol. 8, 2nd ed. Pages 289ff.

Hampe, J. Ch., ed. *Die Autorität der Freiheit: Gegenwart des Konzils und Zukunft der Kirche im ökumenischen Disput.* Vol. 3. Munich: Kösel, 1967.

Hauser, L. "Bedingungen ökumenischer Gespräche in 'nachchristlicher Zeit': Zur Bedeutung von Karl Rahners theologischer Theorie der Moderne." *Una Sancta* 41 (1986): 285–94.

Hegel, G.W.F. *Phänomenologie des Geistes.* Ed. J. Hofmeister. 6th ed. Hamburg: Meiner, 1952.

Heidegger, M. *Kant und das Problem der Metaphysik.* 3rd. ed. Frankfurt am Main: Klostermann, 1965.

———. *Sein und Zeit.* 10th ed. Tübingen: Niemeyer, 1963.

Hilberath, B. J. *Die Problematik des trinitätstheologischen Personenbegriffs (Tertullian–Rahner).* Innsbruck: Kösel, 1986.

Hoerers, W. *Kritik der transzendentalphilosophischen Erkenntnistheorie.* Stuttgart: Kohlhammer, 1969.

———. "Rahner und Kant—Von der Metaphysik zur 'Auslegung der Subjektivität.'" *Theologisches* 185 (1985): 6586–92.

Kant, I. *Kritik der reinen Vernunft.* 4th ed. Ed. W. Weischedel. Frankfurt am Main: Wissenschaftliche Buchgesellschaft, 1975.

Kasper, W. "Karl Rahner: Theologe in einer Zeit des Umbruchs." *Theologische Quartalschrift* 159 (1979): 263–71.
Kaufmann, G. D. "Is There Any Way from Athens to Jerusalem?" *Journal of Religion* 59 (1979): 340–46.
Kern, W. "Karl Rahners *Grundkurs des Glaubens*: Kleine Einführung in eine große Einführung." *Stimmen der Zeit* 102 (1977): 326–36.
Kienzler, K. "Geheimnis Gottes und Transzendentaltheologie. Karl Rahner." *Religionsphilosophie heute.* Eds. A. Halder, K. Kienzler, and J. Möller. Düsseldorf: Patmos, 1988. Pages 162–68.
Klein, W. *Teilhard de Chardin und das zweite Vatikanische Konzil: Ein Vergleich der Pastoralkonstitution über die Kirche in der Welt von heute mit Aspekten der Weltschau Pierre Teilhard de Chardin. Abhandlungen zur Sozialethik.* Vol. 8. Munich: Schöningh, 1979.
Kleindienst, E. *Wege aus dem Säkularismus: Versuche zur Bestimmung des Weges der Kirche in säkularisierter Gesellschaft.* Donauwörth: Auer, 1991.
Klinger, E. "Der Glaube an den Menschen – eine dogmatische Aufgabe. Karl Rahner als ein Wegbereiter des Zweiten Vatikanischen Konzils." *Theologie und Glaube* 75 (1985): 299–338.
Klinger, E., and K. Wittstadt, eds. *Glaube im Prozeß: Christsein nach dem II. Vatikanum—für Karl Rahner.* Freiburg: Herder, 1984.
Krauss, M. "Einweihung in das Geheimnis: Anmerkung zu Karl Rahners Theologie." *Quatember. Vierteljahreshefte für Erneuerung und Einheit der Kirche* 43 (1979): 90–94.
———. "Karl Rahner—Skizzen zur Person." *Quatember. Vierteljahreshefte für Erneuerung und Einheit der Kirche* 48 (1984): 151–54.
———. "Vom Urgeheimnis, das wir Gott nennen: Karl Rahner begeht den 80. Geburtstag." *Lutherische Monatshefte* 23 (1984): 101–3.
Küng, H. "Im Interesse der Sache: Antwort an Karl Rahner." *Stimmen der Zeit* 96 (1971): 43–64, 105–22.

Lakebrink, B. *Klassische Metaphysik: Eine Auseinandersetzung mit der existentialen Anthropozentrik.* Freiburg i. Br.: Rembach, 1967.

Lechner, M. *Die Theologie des Maßes: Studien zur kulturgeschichtlichen Bedeutung der Askese bei Romano Guardini.* St. Ottilien: EOS, 1991.

Lehmann, K. "In memoriam Karl Rahner." Tribute on Bavarian Radio: *Catholic World.* April 1, 1984, 8:00–8:30. Bavarian Radio Telescript from April 1, 1986. Page 5.

———. "Theologie aus Leidenschaft des Glaubens: Gedanken zum Tod von Karl Rahner." *Stimmen der Zeit* 109 (1984): 291–98.

Lehmann, K., and A. Raffelt, eds. *Karl Rahner–Praxis des Glaubens: Geistliches Lesebuch.* Freiburg: Benziger, Herder, 1982.

———. *Rechenschaft des Glaubens: Karl Rahner—Lesebuch.* Freiburg: Benziger, Herder, 1979.

Losinger, A. *"Iusta autonomia": Studien zu einem Schlüsselbegriff des II. Vatikanischen Konzils.* Paderborn: Schöningh, 1989.

———. *Selbstbestimmung des Menschen und der Welt? Anspruch und Grenzen des Autonomiegedankens.* Cologne: Bachem, 1990.

Lotz, J. B. *Transzendentale Erfahrung.* Freiburg: Herder, 1978.

Maréchal, J. *Le point de départ de la métaphysique. Leçons sur le développement historique et théorique du problème de la connaissance.* 3rd ed. Brussells: L'Édition universelle, 1944.

Mette, N. "Zwischen Reflexion und Entscheidung. Der Beitrag Karl Rahners zur Grundlegung der praktischen Theologie." *Trierer Theologische Zeitschrift* 87 (1978): 26–43, 136–51.

Metz, J. B. *Christliche Anthropozentrik: Über die Denkform des Thomas von Aquin.* Munich: Kösel, 1962.

———. "Karl Rahner—ein theologisches Leben." *Stimmen der Zeit* 99 (1974): 305–16.

———. "Karl Rahner zu vermissen: Zur Erinnerung an

den großen Theologen." *Geist und Leben: Zeitschrift für Aszese und Mystik* 59 (1985): 83–87.

———. "Theologie als Biographie." *Concilium* 12 (1976): 311–15.

Metz, J. B., ed. *Gott in Welt: Festgabe für Karl Rahner*. 2 vols. Freiburg: Herder, 1963.

Mitterstieler, E. *Christlicher Glaube als Bestätigung des Menschen: Zur "fides quaerens intellectum" in der Theologie Karl Rahners.* Frankfurter Theologische Studien 18. Frankfurt am Main: J. Knecht, 1975.

Möller, J. "Der späte Heidegger und die Theologie." *Tübiger Theologische Quartalschrift* 147 (1967): 386–431.

———. *Die Chance des Menschen—Gott genannt*. Einsiedeln: Benziger, 1975.

———. *Glauben und Denken im Widerspruch? Philosophische Fragen an die Theologie der Gegenwart*. Munich: E. Wewel, 1969.

———. *Menschsein: Ein Prozeß*. Düsseldorf: Patmos, 1979.

———. *Wahrheit als Problem*. Munich: E. Wewel, 1971.

Moltmann, J. "Christsein, Menschsein, und das Reich Gottes: Ein Gespräch mit Karl Rahner." *Stimmen der Zeit* 110 (1985): 619–31.

Muck. O. *Die transzendentale Methode in der scholastischen Philosophie der Gegenwart*. Innsbruck: F. Rauch, 1964.

Mussner, F. "Christologie—systematisch und exegetisch" [Rezension]. *Theologisch-Praktische Quartalschrift* 122 (1974): 181–84.

Neufeld, K. H. "Theologen und Konzil: Karl Rahners Beitrag zum Zweiten Vatikanischen Konzil." *Stimmen der Zeit* 109 (1984): 156–66.

Neuhaus, G. "Die Einheit von Nächsten- und Gottesliebe: Karl Rahners These vor der Herausforderung durch Feuerbach." *Forum Katholische Theologie* 1 (1985): 176–96.

———. *Transzendentale Erfahrung als Geschichtsverlust: Der Vorwurf der Subjektlosigkeit an Rahners Begriff geschichtlicher*

Existenz und eine weiterführende Perspektive transzendentaler Theologie. Düsseldorf: F. Rauch, 1982.

Neumann, K. *Der Praxisbezug in der Theologie bei Karl Rahner.* Freiburg: Herder, 1980.

Ohlig, K. H. "Impulse zu einer 'Christologie von unten' bei Karl Rahner." In *Wagnis Theologie: Erfahrungen mit der Theologie Karl Rahners (Karl Rahner zum 75. Geburtstag am 5. März, 1979).* Ed. H. Vorgrimler. Freiburg: Herder, 1979. Pages 259–73.

Peters, A. *Befreiungstheologie und Transzendentaltheologie: E. Dussel und K. Rahner im Vergleich.* Freiburger Theologische Studien 137. Tübingen: J C.B. Mohr, 1988.

———. "Zwischen Gottesmystik und Christuszeugnis: Zur Theologie Karl Rahners (5.3.1904–20.3.1984)." *Theologische Rundschau* 51 (1986): 269–314.

Pohlmann, R. "Autonomie." *Historisches Wörterbuch der Philosophie,* Vol. 1. Ed. J. Ritter. Basel: Herder, 1971. Pages 701–19.

Punt, J. *Die Idee der Menschenrechte: Ihre geschichtliche Entwicklung und ihre Rezeption durch die moderne katholische Sozialverkündigung.* Paderborn: F. Schöningh, 1987.

Puntel, L. B. "Zu den Begriffen 'transzendental' und 'kategorial' bei Karl Rahner." In *Wagnis Theologie: Erfahrungen mit der Theologie Karl Rahners (Karl Rahner zum 75. Geburtstag am 5. März, 1979).* Ed. H. Vorgrimler. Freiburg: Herder, 1979. Pages 189–98.

Ratzinger, J. *Einführung in das Christentum.* 3rd ed. Munich: Deutscher Taschenbuch Verlag, 1977.

———. "Vom Verstehen des Glaubens. Anmerkungen zu Rahners *Grundkurs des Glaubens.*" *Theologische Revue* 74 (1978): 177–86.

Scannone, J. C. "Die Logik des Existentiellen und Geschichtlichen nach Karl Rahner." In *Wagnis Theologie: Erfahrungen mit der Theologie Karl Rahners (Karl Rahner zum 75. Geburtstag am 5. März, 1979).* Ed. H. Vorgrimler. Freiburg: Herder, 1979. Pages 82–98.

Schaeffler, R. *Die Wechselbeziehungen zwischen Philosophie und katholischer Theologie.* Darmstadt: Wissenschaftliche Buchgesellschaft, 1980.

Scheffczyk, L. "Christentum als Unmittelbarkeit zu Gott: Erwägungen zu Karl Rahners *Grundkurs des Glaubens.*" *Internationale Kirchliche Zeitschrift,* 6 (1977): 442–50.

———. "Die 'organische' und die 'transzendentale' Verbindung zwischen Natur und Gnade." *Forum Katholische Theologie,* 4 (1988): 161–79.

———. *Einführung in die Seköpfungslehre.* 3rd ed. Darmstadt: Wissenschaftliche Burhgesellschaft, 1987.

Schenk, R. *Die Gnade vollendeter Endlichkeit: Zur transzendentaltheologischen Auslegung der Thomanischen Anthropologie.* Freiburg: Herder, 1988.

Schrofner, E. "Gnade und Erfahrung bei Karl Rahner und Leonardo Boff: Zwei Wege gegenwärtiger Gnadentheologie." *Geist und Leben: Zeitschrift für Aszese und Mystik* 53 (1980): 266–80.

Schweizer, E. "Aspekte der Theologie: Karl Rahners neuer *Grundkurs des Glaubens.*" *Univ* 32 (1977): 389–96.

Schwerdtfeger, N. *Gnade und Welt: Zum Grundgefüge von Karl Rahners Theorie des "anonymen Christen."* Freiburg: Herder, 1982.

Seckler, M. "Einführung in den Begriff des Christentums." *Herder Korrespondenz* 30 (1976): 516–21.

Seeber, D. "Helfer im Glauben: Zum Tode von Karl Rahner." *Herder Korrespondenz* 38 (1984): 220–24.

Simons, E. *Philosophie der Offenbarung in Auseinandersetzung mit "Hörer des Wortes" von Karl Rahner.* Stuttgart: Kohlhammer, 1966.

Splett, J. *Der Mensch ist Person: Zur christlichen Rechtfertigung des Menschseins.* Frankfurt am Main: Knecht, 1978.

Spülbeck, O. "Teilhard de Chardin und die Pastoralkonstitution." In *Die Autorität der Freiheit: Gegenwart des Konzils und Zukunft der Kirche im ökumenischen Disput.* Vol. 3. Ed. J. Ch. Hampe. Munich: Kösel, 1967. Pages 86–97.

Torrance, T. F. "Toward an Ecumenical Consensus on the Trinity." *Theologische Zeitschrift* 31 (1975): 337–50.

Verweyen, H. "Wie wird das Existential übernatürlich? Zu einem Grundproblem der Anthropologie Karl Rahners." *Trierer Theologische Zeitschrift* 95 (1986): 115–31.
Vorgrimler, H. "Ein Brief zur Einführung." In *Wagnis Theologie: Erfahrungen mit der Theologie Karl Rahners (Karl Rahner zum 75. Geburtstag am 5. März, 1979).* Ed. H. Vorgrimler. Freiburg: Herder, 1979. Pages 11–20.
Vorgrimler, H., ed. *Wagnis Theologie: Erfahrungen mit der Theologie Karl Rahners (Karl Rahner zum 75. Geburtstag am 5. März, 1979).* Freiburg: Herder, 1979.
Vorgrimler, H., and J. B. Metz, eds. *Gott in Welt: Festgabe für Karl Rahner zum 60. Geburtstag.* 2 vols. Freiburg: Herder, 1963.
Weger, K. H. "Das 'anonyme' Christentum in der heutigen Theologie." *Stimmen der Zeit* 101 (1976): 319–32.
———. "Zur Theologie Karl Rahners." *Erbe und Auftrag* 63 (1987): 337–48.
Weger, K. H., ed. *Religionskritik von der Aufklärung bis zur Gegenwart: Autoren—Lexikon von Adorno bis Wittgenstein.* Freiburg: Herder, 1979.
Wenisch, B. "Zur Theologie Karl Rahners." *Münchener Theologische Zeitschrift* 28 (1977): 383–97.
Weß, P. "Wie kann der Mensch Gott erfahren? Eine Überlegung zur Theologie Karl Rahners." *Zeitschrift für Katholische Theologie* 102 (1980): 343–48.
Wiederkehr, D. "Chancen und Grenzen anthropologischer Theologie: Zu Karl Rahners *Grundkurs des Glaubens.*" *Wissenschaft und Weisheit* 40 (1977): 197–204.
Wisser, R., ed. *Martin Heidegger im Gespräch.* Freiburg: K. Alber, 1970.
Wood, C. M. "Karl Rahner on Theological Discourse." *Journal of Ecumenical Studies* 12 (1975): 55–67.

Introductory Texts

Heijden, B. van der. *Karl Rahner: Darstellung und Kritik seiner Grundpositionen.* Einsiedeln: Johannes, 1973.

Lehmann, K. "Karl Rahner." In *Bilanz der Theologie im 20. Jahrhundert.* Vol. 4. Eds. H. Vorgrimler and R. van der Gucht. Freiburg: Herder, 1970. Pages 143–80.

———. "Karl Rahner: Ein Porträt." In *Rechenschaft des Glaubens: Karl Rahner—Lesebuch.* Eds. K. Lehmann and A. Raffelt. Freiburg: Herder, 1979. Pages 13*–53*.

Metz, J. B. "Karl Rahner." In *Tendenzen der Theologie im 20. Jahrhundert.* 2nd ed. Berlin: Kreutz, 1967. Pages 513–18.

Speck, J. *Karl Rahners theologische Anthropologie: Eine Einführung.* Munich: Kösel, 1967.

Vorgrimler, H. *Karl Rahner: Leben—Denken—Werke.* Munich: Manz, 1963.

———. *Karl Rahner verstehen: Eine Einführung in sein Leben und Denken.* Freiburg: Herder, 1985.

Weger, K. H. *Karl Rahner: Eine Einführung in sein theologisches Denken.* Freiburg: Herder, 1978.

BIBLIOGRAPHIES AND DICTIONARIES

Bleistein, R. *Bibliographie Karl Rahner, 1969–1974.* Freiburg: Herder, 1974.

Bleistein, R., and E. Klinger. *Bibliographie Karl Rahner, 1924–1969.* With an introduction by H. Vorgrimler. Freiburg: Herder, 1969.

Imhof, P., and H. Biallowons, eds. *Karl Rahner im Gespräch.* 2 vols. Munich: Kösel, 1987.

Imhof, P., and H. Treziak. "Bibliographie Karl Rahner, 1974–1979." In *Wagnis Theologie: Erfahrungen mit der Theologie Karl Rahners (Karl Rahner zum 75. Geburtstag am 5. März 1979).* Ed. H. Vorgrimler. Freiburg: Herder, 1979. Pages 579–97.

Neufeld, K., and R. Blestein. *Rahner-Register: Ein Schlüssel zu Rahners "Schriften zur Theologie I-X" und zu seinen Lexikonartikeln.* Zurich: Benziger, 1974.

Raffelt, A. "Karl Rahner: Bibliographie der Sekundärliteratur, 1948–1978." In *Wagnis Theologie: Erfahrungen mit der*

Theologie Karl Rahners (Karl Rahner zum 75. Geburtstag am 5. März 1979). Ed. H. Vorgrimler. Freiburg: Herder, 1979. Pages 598–622.

Rahner, Karl, ed. *Herders Theologisches Taschenlexikon in acht Bänden.* Freiburg: Herder, 1972.

Rahner, Karl, and H. Vorgrimler. *Kleines Theologisches Wörterbuch.* 11th ed. Freiburg: Herder, 1976.

INDEX

Amelung, E., xxv
Aquinas, Thomas, 19, 78, 81

Balthasar, Hans Urs von, 18, 93
Bantle, F. X., xxv
Biallowons, H., xxvii, 21
Blumenberg, H., xxv
Böckle, F., 48
Bokwa, I., 51
Bonaventure, 33, 34
Brock, Th., 52
Buber, Martin, 93

Copernicus, 19

Daecke, S. M., 52
Descartes, René, xix, xx, 6, 7, 19
Dych, William V., S.J., xxvi, xxvii

Eicher, P., xxiii, xxvi, xxvii, 18, 19, 21, 49

Fabro, C., xxvi, 18
Feuerbach, Ludwig, vii, viii, ix, x, xiv, xx
Fischer, K. P., xxiii, xxvii, 13, 14, 21, 22, 33, 34, 44, 49, 50, 52, 87, 90
Freud, Sigmund, ix

Gadamer, H.-G., xxv
Galling, Kurt, xxv
Greiner, F., 79
Guardini, Romano, xvii, 94
Gucht, R. van der, xxvii, 17

Halder, A., xxv, 22, 49
Hampe, J. Ch., 52
Hegel, G. W. F., vii, viii, ix, 21, 56, 78, 80
Heidegger, Martin, xi, xiii, 7, 8, 10, 11, 12, 13, 18, 19, 20, 36, 81
Hoerers, W., 78, 80
Hume, David, vii, ix, x, 8
Husserl, Edmund, xi

Ignatius of Loyola, 74, 75, 82
Imhof, P., xxvii, 21

Jesus Christ, 24, 41, 42, 43, 44, 45, 47, 51, 52, 72, 73

Kant, Immanuel, vii, ix, x, xi, xii, xiii, xix, xx, 7, 8, 9, 10, 13, 18, 19, 30, 55, 60, 61, 62, 63, 77, 78, 79, 81
Kienzler, K., 22
Kierkegaard, Søren, vii, viii
Klein, W., 52
Kleindienst, E., 18
Krause, Gerhard, xxv
Krauss, M., 22

INDEX OF NAMES CITED

Lakebrink, B., xxvi
Lechner, Michael, 94
Lehmann, K., xxiii, xxvii, 17, 35, 50, 53, 81, 82, 83
Lessing, G. E., 16, 74, 75
Losinger, Anton, xii, xiii, xiv, xxv, 18
Lotz, J. B., 77, 78, 80

Maréchal, J., 7, 9, 20, 61, 78
Marx, Karl, vii, viii, ix, xx
Metz, J. B., xxvi, xxxi, 17, 81
Möller, J., xxvi, 19, 20, 21, 22
Muck, O., 78
Müller, Gerhard, xxv

Nietzsche, F., viii, x, xx

Ohlig, K. H., 51
O'Neill, Michael, xiv

Parmenides, 8, 19
Plato, xi, 8, 82
Pohlmann, R., xxv
Prusak, Bernard, xiv
Punt, J., xxv
Puntel, L. B., 20, 58, 79, 81

Raffelt, A., xvii, 48, 53, 83
Rahner, H., 21

Ratzinger, Joseph, 18, 93, 94
Richardo, Michael, xxvi
Ritter, J., xxv
Rosenzweig, Franz, 91

Scannone, J. C., 82
Schaeffler, R., 78
Scheffczyk, Leo, 2, 3, 18
Schleberger, Eugenie, xiv
Simons, E., xxvi, 90
Splett, J., xxv
Spülbeck, O., 52

Teilhard de Chardin, Pierre, 52
Thysing, W., 51
Troxell, Mary Stephan, xiv

Vogler, Paul, xxv
Vorgrimler, H., xxiii, xxvii, 12, 13, 17, 20, 21, 50

Weger, K. H., xxiii, xxv, xxvii, 5, 12, 18, 21, 23, 36, 47, 48, 49, 50, 71, 73, 81, 82, 90
Wisser, R., 20

Zimmermann, A., 19

www.ingramcontent.com/pod-product-compliance
Lightning Source LLC
Chambersburg PA
CBHW072337300426
44109CB00042B/1654